Pocket Full of Posies

by
Sandra Sweeny Silver

authorHOUSE™

1663 LIBERTY DRIVE, SUITE 200
BLOOMINGTON, INDIANA 47403
(800) 839-8640
WWW.AUTHORHOUSE.COM

First published by AuthorHouse 07/27/05

ISBN: 1-4208-4144-0 (sc)

Library of Congress Control Number: 2005902390

Printed in the United States of America
Bloomington, Indiana

This book is printed on acid-free paper.

Table of Contents

PERENNIAL THOUGHTS

William Blake shouted, "Everything that lives is holy!" I see this truth all around me. But a garden of perennials will day by day, year in and year out teach not only the miracle of all things, but the tenacity and brevity of life itself.

Unlike people, perennials do not despair about the weather. March may bluster, blow and snow, but snowshoe to your perennial garden and you'll see spears of Daffodils and Narcissus, hairy, fat Poppy leaves, cones of Hyacinths and Tulips, tiny blue buds of Scilla siberica and peeking through the "poor man's manure" a circle of Crocus or demure Galanthus. They know it's coming. Try to catch the showy Oriental Poppy pop her pod and unfurl her paper petals. Or try to see the butter-yellow Day Lily uncurl for the day and die at night---forever. Flowers are very private.

Plant a stand of red or pink Bee Balm. In July and August discover the bumblebees, butterflies and hummingbirds dipping their pointy nectar tongues into the tiny recesses of the flower's body. Smell the pungent leaves and flowers. Oswego Tea is made from them. Bees die among this Balm with full nectar crops.

Let the red, ferny Achillea and the white, goose-necked panicles of Strife invade your garden. Let Queen Anne sew her pale lace wherever she wants. Don't discourage Solidago's golden rods, Liatris' furry spikes, the baby Foxgloves huddled close to their dead mother or the wandering children of the Spoon Mum. Give Thyme free rein. They're all teachers.

Beauty, persistence, brevity, continuity, The quiet holiness all around us. We were born in a Garden. Why not birth one?

FIRST FOODS---FIRST FRIENDS: 1620

When the leaky <u>Mayflower</u> floundered on the cold November shores of the New World, the Pilgrims were half-starved, half-crazed and holy grateful. The Spartan stores of biscuits, salted beef and stale beer were almost exhausted. An exploration party led by Miles Standish found baskets of seed corn buried by the Wampanoag Indians in a hill nearby. This sturdy yellow kernel was to become a basic staple not only for the Founding Families but for the whole world.

That first winter the Saints, clinging to the craggy beaches of the new land, died of scurvy, pneumonia, tuberculosis, starvation and ignorance. They were ignorant of the land and its cornucopia of cures, foods and fuels. Then came Spring and Squanto.

This English-speaking Indian had been captured c. 1610 and taken to Plymouth, England. Some think Squanto recrossed the Atlantic with Captain John Smith in 1614. Squanto's routes and roots are vague, but one thing is clear. He was a Godsend for the English settlers. As William Bradford wrote "Squanto was a speciall instrumente sent of God for [our] good and beyond [our] expectation." Squanto not only shared their lives, but within a year he had come to know the God Who had brought the Pilgrims to this land.

As the New England Spring warmed the earth, Squanto taught the Pilgrims how to plant corn for the harvest---four kernels to a hillock. He invited them to taste and to cook the yellow and green squash that the immigrants had thought inedible and the blood red berries in the cranberry bogs that they had felt were poisonous.

He beckoned, "Here is food": herring from the Plymouth Town Brook. "This is food": the red tomatoes that hung from fat stems. (Later the tomato would be considered poisonous until the late 1600's.) "Dig here for food": earthy, long tubers of white potatoes. "Watch. This is the best": strip the bark from this tree and watch the sap leak out. Get buckets. Boil it. Maple syrup. Yum! Even the trees of the New World were good to eat.

All of these foods and hundreds more as we pushed westward were sent back to the Old World as prizes. The white potato so common now in Europe was indigenous to America. When it was introduced to Europe in the 1500's, its journey started in Italy where its arrival coincided with the out-break of a disease. The Italians blamed the pestilence on the potato, so the spud was shoved north where the Germans loved it, the French fried it and the Irish built an economy on it.

All the natural wealth and wonder of America the Bountiful was poured into the Pilgrims by Squanto and the friendly Indians. When the Fall harvest of corn and squash and beans and grapes and berries and nuts was combined with catches of fish and fowl, the Pilgrims invited the Wampanoags to a Thanksgiving to God Feast. The Indians brought five deer and stayed three days. In addition to the venison and vegetables, they ate lobsters, fat eel pies, corn bread and "sallet herbes" from the wild greens. This first Thanksgiving was celebrated in October. Our November date was established by President Abraham Lincoln who made it an official holiday in 1863.

One can imagine the warm Indian Summer sun filtering through the Fall foliage on the First Feast--the Pilgrims with their faith tested and triumphing and the Indians with their innocence wondering and waning. One can imagine the holy sojourners who had braved a New World and the holy hunters who had made them welcome.

WHICH CAME FIRST: THE CHICKEN OR THE EGG?

Which came first: the chicken or the egg? This is really a metaphysical question. If you are a Biblical literalist, anti-evolutionist, I guess you would have to say the chicken came first. God created all matter including chickens fiatly (i.e. He spoke and it was). Everything He created was "seed bearing." Every created living thing contained within itself the ability to reproduce itself. So the chicken came first and then she laid an egg.

Of course, if you are an evolutionist, you would probably never be able sufficiently to tackle the chicken-egg conundrum. Maybe the egg. No the chicken. But... Too many variables. No real place to begin.

When it comes to flower names, it's hard to determine which came first. Was there a girl named Rosemary who was so sweet-smelling and so unforgettable that she bequeathed for all time her unforgettableness to the herb Rosemary? And how influential and scientifically prominent must have been the man who couldn't forget his Rosemary and stamped her name forever on that tender perennial bush! Or did the herb come first and get its name for its signatory scent and then somewhere along the line way back in Roman and then English times did certain parents see their little newborn's tender head and say, "Rosemary. She'll be called Rosemary after that sweet-smelling herb I use in my mutton."? Then other people liked the sound of that name and named their little girls Rosemary, too.

Not many girls are called "Violet" anymore. But it was once bestowed on non-purple girls as was Iris and Daphne and Malva and Pansy---all flower names. Yes, I did know a "Pansy." She was married to a man named G. Six. They lived in One Hundred, Pennsylvania. She would introduce herself as "Pansy Six From a Hundred which leaves Ninety-Four."

Certainly you can't get a more flower name than "Flora." I once knew a Flora whom everyone called "Flo." She had the misfortune to have fallen out of a barn loft onto her head when she was a girl. She was somewhat affected by the experience but always insisted upon being called "Flora." "Hi, Flo," someone would yell. "I'm not Flo! I'm Flora!!" she would bellow back. She may not have had the delicate voice of the flower, but Flo had the delicacy of spirit to know that she bore the name of Beauty.

Blossom is not "in" anymore, but in my childhood I knew a few Blossoms. None of the two I'm recalling reminded me of the fineness and the purity of a blossom, but both of them tended to "open up a little" as they matured.

I have known an Erica (the Heath plant) or two. The ones I've known do seem to have the hardiness and tenacity one needs to cling to a harsh clime.

The three Gingers (the pungent spice) I've known all looked alike. Truly. All three were about 5'3"-5'5" with either natural or enhanced blond hair. They all drank and smoked. They all were very "cute." They were definitely in the popular high school and then country club crowd.

Now "Melissa" means "honeyed." (Melissa is still an "in" name.) The ones I've known are never terribly sweet in the honeyed sense of the word. But boys are drawn to them as bees to honey. One Melissa used to let boys in her bedroom window while her parents were having dinner parties. She would emerge to meet the guests; return to her room; re-emerge for dinner; return to her room and re-re-emerge to bid adieu. Another Melissa always complained that boys only wanted one thing from her. Well, have you ever set out a plateful of honey? Do so on a high-sun summer day and watch the bees swarm around and in and on the plate. Melissa definitely has something desirable.

"Daisy, Daisy. Give me your answer true. I'm half-crazy..." The Daisy I met when she was 90 years old was more than "half-crazy." She was full-crazy. The only way you could stop her from swearing and summoning demonic spirits was to start singing, "Daisy, Daisy. Give me your answer true." I've never known another Daisy, so I'm sure this Daisy was not typical. But I wonder. If you were named Daisy would you be indecisive? Loves me; loves me not; loves me; loves me not. Or would a Daisy be commonly beautiful as are her namesakes who clothe the highways of America with their white beauty?

I haven't known an Ivy. Would she be clinging and tenacious as is the wonderful, almost unkillable ivy? Would she be the kind of mother who wraps herself so tightly around her husband and children that she would eventually have to be removed forcefully? Or would she choose to trail herself around the periphery of their lives in such a way that she is thought of as steady and reliable? I don't know.

The one Veronica I knew did look like a well-endowed Veronica plant. She was tall and had an over-all pointy appearance. Her hair was always in place and so were her clothes. She seemed to know where she was going.

I've known a dog named Holly and a woman named Holly. The dog was so-named because he was a Christmas present. He was a small, miniature pug with a saliva problem. The woman named Holly was a very expansive personality who was always giving fun parties. It was Christmas every month. One party she gave was a Bad Taste Party. Everyone was supposed to come and do something in bad taste. I dressed in Connecticut pink and green which I considered in bad taste. Some came dressed in their p.j.'s. I think they thought it was a Pajama Party. Some brought half-eaten pizza. But my husband got the award for The Worst Bad Taste. He dressed in a suit and carried around his guitar in its cumbersome case. He mingled normally but fondled various parts of people's anatomy with his guitar case as he mingled. He kept saying, "Excuse me. Oh, I'm sorry. May I get through?" His bad taste was so subtle that he ended up alienating a small portion of the crowd among whom was Holly's husband's boss's wife.

She came to Holly and said she and her husband were leaving. Holly found out it was because Steve was repeatedly brushing his guitar against her. She tried to explain that he was doing it because it was a Bad Taste Party. The woman was not convinced. They left. Steve got his Award and Holly's husband was transferred and given a promotion within six months.

One of the flowering plants I love most is the Marguerite. It is sturdy, reliable and filled with hundreds of yellow or white daisies. It's a mainstay in the summer garden. I knew one Marguerite years ago in Lausanne, Switzerland. She was a German girl with dark eyes and dark hair and had one of the sweetest dispositions of anyone I've ever known. She had become a Christian and she glowed. When I see my Marguerites beaming in the summer sun, I occasionally think of Marguerite.

Both of the Heathers I've known were relatively tall and had brown hair. The Heathers (and the Heaths) are some of my favorite small shrub plants. I have a garden of just heaths, heathers and thymes. The trio work very well together. The thymes spread all over and the heaths and heathers can be staggered in bloom and in color so that you can have a gray, green, red and rust color almost all year long. The two Heathers are both colorful ladies. One likes to wear strange and funny hats and the other likes to disappear for long periods of time. But they are both survivors like my Heathers.

Of course, there are a lot of Roses. That's probably the most common flower name for girls. The rose is considered by those in the know to be the queen of flowers. Antoine de St. Exupery made the rose the symbol of woman on the planet <u>The Little Prince</u> tried so hard to keep running smoothly. In that charming allegory the little prince's rose is always complaining about something. He has such a time trying to keep her happy. Aristocratic, fussy, hard to take care of, incomparable---that's the rose's reputation.

I've known some Roses in my time. One left her three children when they were young, went to California and re-married a pervert who molested one of her grandchildren. Another Rose was a waitress in a coffee shop who slid your mug at warp speed and then laughed when it abruptly stopped all over someone's ham and eggs. Another Rose would give you the shirt off her back and married a man who gave her the shirt off his back. They were the happiest couple and had the type of home you loved to go to. Another Rose was delicately beautiful and had such a delicate constitution that she took to her bed for weeks at a time. Her father found her a strapping young man. She married him and every year or so they had another baby. She ended up running her husband, her children and a small craft shop.

Most of the men who bear the names of flowers are mythical or have been dead a long time: Adonis, Achilles, Endymion and that fellow who drowned looking at himself, Narcissus. We have extrapolated a lot from that incident in mythology. You heard little about Narcissus until the rise of modern psychology, "study of the psyche or soul." The Narcissistic personality was definitely a twentieth century phenomenon. If you are that type, you are "self" or "soul"-centered. Think back on literature. How many Narcissistic personalities are depicted? Not many. There are money-grubbers like Silas Marner. There are silly ones like Tom Jones. There are greedy ones like Shylock. There are mean ones like Fagan. But there are few navel-gazers with the exception of Hamlet. Navel-gazing seems to be the privilege, almost the prerogative, of post-20th century people.

So---do we become what we becalled? There are countless people who have changed their names in order to try to change who they are. Would I become taller if I changed my name to Allium Giganteum? Would I become shorter if I changed my name to Mignonette? Would my hair be curly rather than straight if I changed my name to Parsley? Would I be a more profound thinker if I changed my name to Cosmos? Would I have had more children if my name had been Fructescens rather than Sandra? Who knows?

I think the whole name/identification question is like the chicken/egg query. You can argue it either way.

VEGETABLE HASH AND TWO DEEP-DISH APPLE PIES: THE GOOD, OLD LIFE

Personal diaries are rarely considered high literature. When they survive, their worth to future generations are usually as historical source books for facts, anecdotes, scandals and the atmosphere of the period. Diaries, also, often preserve for us little-known people whose scribblings mirror our own needs and aspirations. Samuel Pepys' (1635-1703) diary is perhaps the most interesting and readable example we have. John Evelyn (1620-1706), best known for his diary, left a rather dull but reliable source of information about English mores and court life in the 17th century.

My son gave me a book for Christmas---<u>New England Year</u> by Muriel Follett. This gentle diary chronicles everyday happenings on a large farm outside of Brattleboro, Vt. in the year of the Great Hurricane of 1938. Muriel, wife to Rob and mother to 12 year-old Bobby and 10 year-old Jean, was encouraged to record her year by The Stephen Daye Press in Brattleboro: "[they] persuaded me to believe that people would be more interested in what a farmer's life is honestly like than in any story I might make up. I hope [they're] right!" They must have been right because this diary of the work, play, hopes and failures of their lives was reissued by Yankee Magazine Publications in 1988---almost 50 years after its first publication.

What resonates in this journal is how much things have changed. World War II is several wars behind us now, but in 1938 the Green Mountain boys had not sailed for European and Pacific theaters. She speaks occasionally of "the European crisis," but the sound of goosesteps did not occupy their minds. The fact that "Christmas is outlawed in Germany" causes her to tell the children how fortunate they are to be allowed to observe the Lord's Birth. But it causes no shudders. Those sensations are reserved for the death of a child from pneumonia or for the wind that seeps into every nook and cranny in the winter and propels the four closer to the cozy stove.

She gives an impromptu review of the premiere of Snow White: "The movie was good...but I was vaguely disappointed in places, mostly because of the jerky unreality of Snow White, the Prince and the Queen." In his diary Samuel Pepys thought Shakespeare's Twelfth Night "but a silly play" and the London production of A Midsummer Night's Dream "the most insipid ridiculous play that ever I saw in my life." So much for the taste of diarists.

Mrs. Follett does give a prescient critique of Roosevelt's emerging Welfare State. "The people who have nothing and have no initiative to get ahead are paid a good salary by the Government to do nothing.... Thousands of good men are lost that way." And "As always the indomitable courage and independence of our Vermont people impresses me....our system strives to help people help themselves. Many of the New Deal dependents would be put to shame if they could see the willing sacrifices and careful planning of people to give their children the advantages of good health and good education." Vermont's rugged individualism and especially the entrepreneurship of a farmer's life were decidedly at odds with the newest deal.

Eating patterns in this part of America have definitely changed in the last 75 years! Those were the good old days. The diary chronicles day after day, month after month of high-fat, high-cholesterol, damn-the-torpedoes-desserts-are-ahead foods. Good food. Wholesome food. American food eaten with thankfulness rather than with guilt.

"Tonight we had oyster stew followed by baked beans, sour-milk biscuits with butter and cheese followed by thick slabs of ice cream and cookies and coffee." Chocolate cakes are baked three times a week and the whole double-decker cake is consumed by the four of them at the end of a hearty meal. One modest family meal of vegetable hash is crowned by two deep-dish apple pies. During strawberry season the four of them eat an "enormous shortcake with three quarts of strawberries on top topped with thick whipped cream."

And being Vermonters, maple sugar syrup drips from mounds of morning pancakes and mingles with thick strips of bacon. Maple candies dot their day and sugaring dominates their Spring lives. Maple syrup is made by tapping maple trees and boiling the sap. It's a long, strenuous process not for the weak. The book jacket says Mrs. Follett, probably clogged with glucose and cholesterol, was still living and active in Vermont in 1988. She would be in her mid to late 80's. One must watch one's diet.

Her diary propels the reader along at a leisurely gait. There are no traumas, no revelations, no suspense. She's not poetic although her choices of material suggest a sensitive, intelligent mother and wife. She is attuned enough to appreciate the steady rhythm of their lives and its inextricable bond to the earth and the seasons. The calving in cold barns, the midnight milking, the canning on hot days, the planting, tending, harvesting, building, repairing---all the small rigors of farm life yesterday and today are here.

On May 1, 1938 she says they found a hole in the earth where a Revolutionary War family had once built a home. "Now nothing is standing but a few foundation stones....It made me feel sad to think of the end of all their hopes and planning. Even the road that used to run by their house has long since been abandoned and is now only a lane through a pasture."

As I read this slice of the past, I feel about her what she felt for that family. And I know that 50-100 years from now someone will feel for me and for my time that same wistful nostalgia.

New England Year: A Journal of Vermont Farm Life, by Muriel Follett, A Yankee Magazine Publication, Dublin, New Hampshire, 1988

THREE BEAR PORRIDGE

I just had the best dinner!

I often ask people, "If you could only have one thing to eat for the rest of your life, what would it be?" I've found the answer depends a lot on the age of the respondents. Those twelve and under tend to answer: "hamburgers," "pizza," "macaroni and cheese," "spaghetti." They like the basics. Between twelve and fifty the responses tend to be more upscale: "lobster," "filet mignon," "filet of lemon sole," "artichokes." There's always a large contingent of people who choose their mother's chicken and dumplings, or her lasagna or her roast beef with mashed potatoes and gravy, or her lemon meringue pie. And then there are the people who don't know what I'm asking and respond, "What do you mean for the rest of my life?" or "Why could I only eat one thing?" or "Do you mean one food or one category of food or what?" or "If I only ate one food, I'd die, wouldn't I?"

The answer to the last question is "no." There is a tribe in Ethiopia who exists solely on beetles. And I've known two mothers who have insisted that their sons have lived for years on only hot dogs. I've also known mothers who claimed their children never ate anything!

What I'm really asking is: What is your favorite food?

Mine is Three Bear Porridge. Three Bear Porridge is a form of Potato Soup.

The Irish love their potatoes. My maiden name is Sweeny (they came to America long before the Potato Famine) which may explain my affinity for the porridge, but my mother didn't have a drop of Irish blood in her and she is the one who "invented" Three Bear Porridge.

One day when my sister, Tooie, and I were about two and a half and four, my mother didn't have any cans of Campbell's soup for our lunch. She decided to make Potato Soup, but she knew that if we knew it was Potato Soup, we'd hate it.

So she boiled some potatoes, celery leaves, and onions in water. She mashed them all up so we couldn't tell there were potatoes in there. She added some milk, salt and pepper and put a big pat of butter on top that melted into yummy circles. We eyed the offering with suspicion.

"What is that?" I grumbled.

"Why, it's...it's the porridge the three bears ate. It's Three Bear Porridge," she improvised. And that's how plebian old Potato Soup (not so proletariat when it's cold and given the French name Vichyssoise) became my favorite food. If I had to, I could live on it.

People fifty to one hundred years old tend to become minimalists where food is concerned and the older they are, the more less is more. Salads are big. Desserts are big. One elderly couple ate oyster stew three times a week and had bacon and tomatoes on lettuce the other four days. Another woman ate peanut butter on bread every day interspersed with an occasional piece of pie.

I gravitate to grilled cheese sandwiches. I think the older you become the more you go for comfort foods, foods that you like and which "mean" something to you.

When she was older, my mother who invented Three Bear Porridge always declined our invitations to go out to dinner. "I've eaten all those foods. You young people go ahead and have a good time." When we'd come home, I'd find she had made herself a sandwich and was curled up with a good book.

I guess I'll be that way, too.

"No, thanks," I'll say to them. "I'll just make myself some Three Bear Porridge and read a little." When they come home, I'll say, "I just had the best dinner!"

For the Recipe for Three Bear Porridge, see:
<u>The Trust Me On This Really Good Food Cook Book,</u>
Sandra Sweeny Silver
Amazon.com; Barnes and Noble.com

THE SECOND LAW OF THERMODYNAMICS

Don't you just hate the Second Law of Thermodynamics? It messes everything up.

I have many friends who are gardeners. When they were in their thirties (often the decade one becomes interested in gardening), they dug and planted and redug and double dug and transplanted and lugged and plugged and did all the heavy work themselves. As their forties and fifties and sixties and seventies relentlessly arrived, they found their knees hurt, their backs broke, their hands cramped, their legs gave out. That's one of the things the Second Law of Thermodynamics means: systems change.

The Second Law of Thermodynamics states that any closed system such as the universe or a body or a garden has a growing tendency toward disorder at the price of order. You can see how this Law invades every area of our lives, environments and minds. Those bodies that begin creeping toward disorder don't work as well as when they were more ordered. This relentless crawl toward disorder is called "entropy."

So instead of saying, "The reason I have a garden helper now is because my knees are gone," you could save your pride and say, "Mary complements my entropic tendencies."

As I see it, entropy is just the result of Original Sin. In the Garden everything was perfect. There were no thorns or thistles and Adam and Eve were meant to live forever. Along came Serpent Satan and beguiled Eve with the possibility of knowledge. She offered the fruit to Adam and he took it immediately. That's always bothered me. How fast Adam fell! He didn't give any objections like Eve did. Eve said to the Serpent, "But God said we'd die if we ate of the fruit of that tree." She, at least, put up some arguments.

The Bible says, and I believe it, that she gave the fruit to Adam and "he ate." (Genesis 3:6) Just like that. No protestations. "He ate." So that First Couple forfeited Eden and eternal physical life and plunged us all into entropy. Death entered and with it the Second Law of Thermodynamics. That Law is associated with the forward movement of Time. And it's that forward movement of Time that makes you look for those ads in the newspaper which bring Mary into your garden every Tuesday.

The Law is at work in our gardens, too. Whether you or you and Mary or professional gardeners tend your garden, very soon the order begins ever so subtly to disintegrate. Your evening primroses have suddenly begun to send up little rosettes one, two or three feet away from where they're supposed to be blooming their little yellow heads off. Everyone knows that if you plant forget-me-nots in the front of your garden, next year they could be in your kitchen! They have no memory whatsoever.

Gooseneck strife and prairie queen and sweet woodruff and violets have no sense of order. They almost define entropy. The day you get your garden just the way you want it---boom! The Second Law of Thermodynamics kicks in.

But it's not just invasives that cause the disintegration into disorder. A very orderly plant like an iris can cause problems. Go out on a balmy Spring day when the first of your irises is blooming. Oh, the smell! The very sight of this stately, ruffled beauty! You wish you had hundreds of them. But go out a week or two later. The delicate ruffles have collapsed into a brownish, gooey ball that blights the whole area. Even later in the season you're down on your knees with clippers cutting back the browning spears of leaves. Unsightly. Entropy. Disorder.

And your prim, orderly roses? They are, hands down, the most entropic of plants. When I first got into gardening, I wanted a modest (12-14 plants) section of roses. I'd sit on my tilting lawn chair and watch them for hours. But I couldn't just watch them I found out. If I wanted to actually HAVE roses, I had to patrol them. I got a bug catcher for the 1st of July arrival of the Japanese beetles. That didn't work, so I got a mayonnaise jar. Day after day I'd go from rose to rose scooping the rose-drugged beetles into the jar. It was almost a full-time job. I had punched holes in the lid to "give the bugs a chance." They died anyway, of course, because they couldn't get out. At the end of several weeks I had a jar full of foul-smelling bugs and every morning hundreds more arrived thinking they had found a pristine feeding ground.

That's when I turned to the deadly sprays. If you read the directions on the side of these insecticides, you know that you are shortening your life by maybe a year or two in order to have a perfect, ordered garden. That year I used the white powder on my prizes right before I left for Cleveland to visit my sister, Tooie. I put a towel around my nose and mouth and gloved my hands, but I was sure the poison had invaded my efforts. I told my three children, "If I seem strange on the trip, have me pull the car over." Of course, this terrified them all the way to Cleveland. But you do have to take health and super-human risks to stave off entropy. The following year, however, I let the Japanese beetles get their roses, the deer got theirs and there were several left over for me.

There are some people who like a casual, disordered garden. I find glory in the weeded OR the wild garden. But no matter what you like, that Second Law of Thermodynamics will be at work. The weeded garden will always tend toward the wild and the wild garden will always revert to Nature. As long as there is death, there will be a progression toward chaos.

But the greatness of gardeners is that even though they know that immutable laws are arrayed against them, they still strive day in and day out for--Beauty.

Against such, there is no law.

Anyway, it's an immutable truth that:

"He who bends to himself a joy
Doth the winged life destroy.
But he who kisses the joy as it flies.
Lives in eternity's sunrise."

William Blake

NOTES ON A FEW WOMEN WHO GOT DIRT UNDER THEIR FINGERNAILS

RUTH STOUT

When someone is always looking outward for joy, satisfaction, riches, meaning or love, there is a saying, "There's acres of diamonds in your own backyard." This adage captures the truism that what you seek is often near at hand.

When we moved to Ridgefield, Connecticut Ruth Stout was already well-known for her organic and year-round gardening. When I got into gardening, I talked to several women who had made the pilgrimage to her garden in Redding, Connecticut right here in our own backyard. And a pilgrimage it was. She was revered in the burgeoning organic food movement. "How did you like Ruth's garden?" They all said, "Her garden is a mess! It stinks!"

The revolutionary method Ruth Stout practiced was this. She planted vegetables. Then she heaped salt hay on the garden to keep down the weeds and hold in the moisture and heat. On top of the salt marsh hay she threw the leavings from her table. Over the years there were many layers of warm hay and kitchen refuse. In January Ruth would snowshoe out to her garden, rummage about in the hay and come back with some carrots, onions, potatoes and broad beans for dinner. She had created an outdoor greenhouse. Voila---year-round gardening.

So why don't we all garden like my famous neighbor used to do? Because her garden was a mess and it stank and those of us who like to grow vegetables also like a modicum of order and good air.

But if you want acres of vegetables in your own backyard, if you are dedicated to gardening in the dead of winter, Ruth Stout is your mentor. She went where no man dared go and few have followed.

<u>Gardening Without Work</u>, Ruth Stout

ELEANOR PERENYI

A Hungarian transplant to America, writer and gardener Eleanor Perenyi has really thrust her hands into our fertile soil. I've peered through the iron gates into her garden in Stonington, Connecticut and thought, "Gee, it's not all that great." In fact, it was heartening to see her somewhat uninspiring, mostly shade garden.

But if you are a writer like Eleanor and you happen to garden, you will eventually write about gardens whether yours is a showcase or not.

Ms. Perenyi was managing editor of <u>Mademoiselle</u> magazine and wrote among other things a book about Liszt, <u>Liszt: The Artist As Romantic Hero.</u>

Her garden book, <u>Green Thoughts,</u> doesn't pretend to be the final book on gardening, but it is filled with no-nonsense observations by an intelligent woman.

Listen.

Re: Chinese Paintings

"Paintings of Chinese gardens in which exquisitely clad ladies (with bound feet) float about tending to potted peonies depict scenes less idyllic than they appear. What we are seeing is a...floral cage."

Re: Flat-leaf Parsley

"No food snob today will use anything but the flat-leafed Italian variety which they have been assured is superior in flavor to the curly-leafed. Well, I don't agree. I much prefer the curly kind...frizzled to accompany fish or croquettes, grated in a Mouli, heaped on a platter for decoration."

Re: The Craze for Fraises des Boises (Wild Strawberries)

"Their flavor isn't a patch on that of a fat, home-grown strawberry of American ancestry. And the gardener who serves them, whether he mentions it or not, has gone through hell to harvest them."

Get the book for a writer's romp through the garden.

GEORGIA O'KEEFFE

William Blake, 18th century artist, poet and lover of God, said, "There is a world in a grain of sand." Georgia O'Keeffe, 20th century artist and eccentric, brought the world of beauty and delight which inhabits the bowels of flowers to the attention of a laconic world. Her blood-red, sensual paintings of the delicate body of the poppy pushed people into the infinity of minute creations.

When Georgia O'Keeffe got off the train in 1929 in Santa Fe, N.M., she immediately felt at home. She was already an established artist whose bold abstractions were selling well in New York at her husband Alfred Steiglitz' Gallery 291. The burgeoning artists' colonies of Taos and Santa Fe were to be her home from then until her death in her '90's.

Late in her life she would be spotted stalking the desert in leather skirts and boots seeking bare bones and rare flowers. Her <u>Skull With Roses</u> (1931), an oil on canvas, depicts a white, bare, animal breastbone with two white calico roses---the living among the dead. She thrust her fingers deep into the hot sand to get that one!

Those Sante Fe artists didn't want to be influenced by other artists. They wanted to paint only what they saw. But the desert is a sparse place. Most of the artists "saw" the same things. Rebecca Salisbury James' <u>Magnolia</u> reverberates O'Keeffe and Raymond Jonson. O'Keeffe's <u>Black Cross</u> has echoes in the works of many other Abstract and Transcendental painters.

But no one shoved our face into a flower like that bold bohemian Georgia. Her paintings of flower faces draw the museum browser, the greeting card industry and the advertising world. She may have loved the bones and bleakness of the desert, but it is for her florid flowers she will be remembered.

She made sure that the adage, "Many a rose is destined to bloom and lose its fragrance on the desert air," didn't apply to her desert.

Becoming O'Keefe: The Early Years, Sharon W. Peters

Georgia O'Keefe, Lisa Mintz Messinger

LADY BIRD JOHNSON

Claudia "Lady Bird" Taylor Johnson said of her first meeting with Lyndon Johnson (she was 21; he was 26): "He was the most outspoken, straight-forward, determined young man I have ever met. I knew I had met something remarkable, but I didn't know quite what." He proposed to her 24 hours later. They married within months and he began to use her father's money to go into politics.

But this isn't about LBJ, however fascinating and complex a man he was. This is about Lady Bird and wildflowers. Every First Lady, and she did live up to her name with her unfailing politeness, has to have a pet project. Lady Bird's was promoting and preserving the free and wild flowers of America.

It is to some degree because of her promotion of a litter-free and environmentally healthy America that the Wildflower Meadow has become so popular. I have tried two. Both looked okay the first year---lots of yarrow, ox-eye daisies, black-eyed Susans; some pinks, bee balm and wild phlox and a few coneflowers, lupines and cosmos. The second year the ox-eyes were everywhere, the lupines had migrated to the side of the road and---well, you know what I mean if you've tried a wildflower meadow.

But do try one. Get a book that tells about preparation and seeding. You don't really need a meadow. Just designate a part of your property as "wild." (Unless it's all designated "wild.")

Here's a list of the 10 Best Seeds To Sow: gaillardia pulchella, aster novae-angliae, chrysanthemum leucanthemum, rudebeckia hirta, echinacea purpurea, coreopsis tinctoria, oenothera biennis, asclepias tuberosa, coreopsis lanceolata, helianthus augustifolius.

Take a chance. Tame a tiger. Go wild. Lady Bird did and look where it got her!

Lady Bird Johnson Wildflower Center---www.wildflower. org/

CONSTANCE SPRY

Constance Spry (1886-1960) is perhaps the only woman who has become famous just because she made great bouquets. She never liked to be called a flower arranger or a florist. She was a "flower decorator" and her floral decorations in windows of swanky London shops got her career started.

How she climbed into the history books on Flower Arranging may be hard for 21st century arrangers to imagine.

Her style is not in vogue today. The arrangements were formal, pedestal-type ones heavily influenced by Dutch and Flemish painters. She emphasized complementary colors rather than contrasting ones and the use of eccentric foliage,

Ms. Spry broke a lot of rules of the time. In her day the vogue was "twelve carnations and some asparagus fern." The formality of her line and mass creations have heavily formed the Traditional school of arranging and even, to a degree, influenced Ikebana.

But flowers in a vase. How elementary. How easy. Yes? No. As anyone who has ever gathered a bunch of blooms will attest, there is an art to putting the stems one by one into a container until you and everyone who sees the result would exclaim, "As pretty as a picture. Constance herself couldn't have done a better job."

Flower Decoration, Constance Spry

ELLEN BIDDLE SHIPMAN

Lots of decorating magazines are periodically full of the new/old style---Arts and Crafts. It's characterized by hand-hewn and made furniture and accessories arranged in a somewhat colonial, folksy, dense and artistically cluttered way.

Ellen Biddle Shipman (1869-1950), the first nationally recognized female landscape designer, took the European formality out of the gardens of the rich and famous in the middle of the 20th century and created with flowers a distinctly colonial American look. Heavily influenced by the artists and craftsman of the Arts and Crafts Movement living around her in Cornish, New Hampshire, she designed lush gardens rich in texture and density, reminiscent, as she said, of the "idealized Grandmother's garden."

She loved and used the heirloom plants: early and late narcissus, tulips, iris, columbines, peonies, foxglove, anchusa, lupine, lemon lilies, larkspur, hollyhocks, asters, day lilies, helenium, boltonia. She emphasized mass plantings for fullness and specific plantings for continual bloom.

The more I read about her style, the more it reminds me of the traditional English perennial border---lazy, lush, languid and lasting.

After all, after 5,000 years of gardening, there are only two types of gardens: the weeded (formal, patterned) and the wild (informal, casual).

Solomon said 3,000 years ago, "There's nothing new under the sun." But Ellen must have really combined the old in a new way. None of her actual gardens survive, but her imagination has. And that imagination has made her famous.

The Gardens of Ellen Biddle Shipman, Judith B. Tankard

TASHA TUDOR

Tasha Tudor, writer and illustrator of almost 100 children's books, is an American original. Maybe "original" is not the right word. Her southern Vermont home is filled with antique birdcages. She cooks on an antique coal stove, serves on antique dishes and every morning puts on an expensive antique dress (c. 1830) to do her chores. An original? Maybe a copy of a 19th century life which does qualify her as an eccentric.

Born in 1914 to a well-connected Boston family (she says she was born into "a state of genteel poverty"), she had a Scottish nanny who extolled the virtues of living off the land, gardening and spinning your own yarn.

Tasha married, had children, wrote books and with time turned into the Tasha Tudor people know and love. Her gardens are legendary. Hopefully the following quotes will whet your appetite for this homespunner.

"I enjoy doing housework, ironing, washing, cooking, dishwashing. Whenever I get one of those questionnaires and they ask what is your profession, I always put down housewife. It's an honorable profession, why apologize for it!"

Posing in her antique gowns, she says, "Why do women want to dress like men when they're fortunate enough to be women?"

"I never use a bulb planter. Those are the most ridiculous things! They sell them to ladies in garden catalogues and you're supposed to dig one little hole at a time. I make several large holes all around and put quite a few daffodils in. That's why it makes such a spectacular look when they bloom."

"Gardening has untold rewards. You never have to go on a diet. At age 76 I can still wear my wedding dress and still chin myself. I've never been depressed

in my whole life and I've never had a headache....I attribute it all to goat's milk and gardening."
    Goat's milk?!

A Brighter Garden, Tasha Tudor

Private World Of Tasha Tudor, Tasha Tudor

MARTHA STEWART

Martha Stewart. The name usually evokes, first of all, a big uh-oh. Enough said. But even before all that, Martha was provocative. She is disdained among some high-achieving women and evokes a little guilt in most women. Why? Because, let's face it, Martha does the little things, the inconsequential things perfectly.

I had never read her books or seen her TV show. Last Christmastime I happened upon her show on the Food Channel and watched her. That woman is amazing! I don't care how many researchers and staff she has. Every thing they propose she masters and manages to make easy enough for you and me to do.

Who says spending two hours making chocolate leaves and twigs to decorate a Christmas cake is silly?

Who says spending four hours to decorate a wreath for your home is dumb?

Who says making cookies the size of Frisbees and wrapping them like they've never been wrapped before and going from door to door in your neighborhood presenting them as Holiday gifts is a waste of time? Who says that?!

Certainly no gardener worth her salt would say spending five hours on her knees under a cold April sun weeding a tangled Spring garden is a waste of time! And no gardener would consider it silly to spend four hours pruning out the dead and dying twigs and branches from azalea bushes.

Are not the inconsequential and the so-called frivolous just those things that make a home a home, that raise children and tend a marriage? Will we all not be known and later judged and remembered for the aggregate of all those small things that gradually build up to make a life?

Hail, Martha! Keep wasting our time! (Hope your "time" was redeemed!)

Gardening, Martha Stewart

Entertaining, Martha Stewart

Hand Made Christmas, Martha Stewart

BARE BONES

My great-grandmother. Her name was Clementine Louys Besancon. She was French. Her grandchildren called her Meme. Her children called her a religious fanatic. I, who never knew her, call her a sister in the Lord.

Bare bones, black dress, Baptist she was. She clung fiercely to the rocky soil of early Ohio and to the Rock of Ages. Her granddaughter, Carmen, my mother, was drawn to her austerity and to her detachment from worldly things. Her daughter, Eunice, my grandmother, was drawn to the bright colors and the allures of Vanity Fair.

"Meme (accent on the "e's") made the best soup, Sandy," Mother would say. "It was, of course, a very plain soup as she considered any show not becoming a Christian woman. But I loved it. She had a garden. It was her only vanity. Lush, full, a riot of color and tumbling blossoms. She would do her chores and then spend whatever time she had left over in the garden. She would prune and dress and drape the plants and shrubs. She would work and then stand back to admire it. As I said, her garden was her only vanity. And she had herbs at her back door. She would heat some milk. Then she would open the back door and snip off some fresh parsley. She and I would sit at the tan wooden kitchen table sipping this delicious white soup peppered with green herb."

I would have added some salt, pepper and butter to this bare-bones broth, but I am a lot spicier than either my mother or my great-grandmother. There are many bloodlines between me and Meme.

My mother made wonderful soups. My passion for soups comes from her. She made vegetable soup (her vegetable soup is the mark, the plumb line for our son Blake). She loved lima bean and split pea soup. A classic potato soup which she called Three Bear Porridge is, as I've indicated, my favorite soup in the whole wide world. I make that Porridge if I am happy or sad; if it is cold outside or too hot; if it is midnight or morning; if I am sick or well.

We lived in Edinburgh, Scotland for a year. I studied Shakespeare at the University of Edinburgh and my husband Steve studied Theology at the New School. Kathy and Blake went to elementary school in our suburb of Costorphine. At the time there was an art gallery in Edinburgh, the DeMarco Art Gallery, owned by a fortyish man who loved artists especially those who went to the Island of Skye to paint clouds.

We would go to the Gallery on weekends with the children to eat lunch at the little restaurant tucked into the basement of the building. Their best soup was Chicken Bone Soup. Girls in their early twenties who longed to marry artists would take the bones from cooked chickens. Then they would boil them for several days until they became soft enough to mash. That was the base and broth from which they made their delicious vegetable soup.

Meme's Parsley Soup and the DeMarco Gallery Chicken Bone Soup are primitive soups. They go way back. They are part of our "Waste not--Want Not" past as are Lentil Soups, Onion Soups, Potato Soups. We have fancied up these types of basic soups, but way back then (and even in some places now) soup was just water flavored with beans, grains, vegetables or herbs.

When I was eighteen and lived in Lausanne, Switzerland, Mme. Simone made our lunch and dinner soups at the Pensione from whatever meat she was serving. The decent, thin, brown liquid in our shallow, white soup bowls was just the meat drippings with water added. I know that now, but I wondered how every day Mme. Simone produced such a tasty broth. Occasionally Mme. would throw some farina in the broth to make it heartier or clip some herbs from the pots by her back door. At eighteen, I thought she was pretty old, but looking back, she was a woman in her late thirties with two young children. She took in two boarders and fed twelve others twice a day. She and her two children lived in one bedroom of the apartment. A brooding girl from Zurich and I lived in her other two bedrooms. Her living room was the dining hall. She had placed a long table in the middle of the room. We all showed up five times a week at 11:30 for dejeuner (lunch) and at 6:00 for souper (dinner). Each meal started with broth and bread. We would have soup, meat, vegetable and salad for lunch and soup, meat and salad for dinner. Her desserts were plain and delicious. Thin puddings like a Crème Anglaise. A sparsely sweetened Apple Tart.

There is another bare-bones soup called Stone Soup. This one has to be ancient. It's really a vegetable soup, but you start with several large gray STONES. These are boiled for a long time in a pot. That particular and peculiar flavoring becomes the broth into which you put whatever vegetables your garden yields.

Bare-bones soups from bare-bones times and people. Drippings and broths and flavored waters are even now the bases of most good soups. For me, soups, the fruits of our labor in the earth mixed with a little water or milk, are one of the bare-bones bases of life.

THE GARDENER'S YEAR

JANUARY
Pussy willows and forsythia can be forced now in a sunny window.

Cut back leggy house plants and then take a long walk in the snow.

FEBRUARY
Order the newest varieties of day lilies from the garden catalogues.

Make a huge pot of old-fashioned, beef-laden vegetable soup for dinner.
Serve it with a crusty, crunchy bread.

MARCH
Prune your blueberries and your grapevines.

Send a spring bouquet to someone who needs to know there's hope.

APRIL
Divide your hostas and day lilies during a warm Spring shower. Get wet.

After the forsythia has flowered is the time to apply crab grass control.

MAY
When planting your vegetable garden, know that beans and salad vegetables will tolerate some shade.

Take time to smell each one of your flowers.

JUNE

Go out in the country to a big farm and pick those sweet strawberries. Make a whole dinner of just strawberry shortcakes.

Use lots of fresh herbs in your salad dressings.

JULY

Pick a bunch of Queen Anne's lace. Put them in a vase of colored water. Watch the white lace turn green, red, blue...

Before lunch, pick ordinary orange day lilies. Stuff them with fresh fruit or with a colorful pasta salad. Invite a friend over to eat your flower fantasia.

AUGUST

Take the pink petals off of a Purple Coneflower. Comb your hair with its sturdy cone.

Have a dinner of just beefsteak tomatoes and Launcelot corn on the cob with lots of butter, salt and pepper.

SEPTEMBER

Mass four or five buckets of mums together at the entrance to your home.

Gather one last HUGE bouquet and give it away to someone.

OCTOBER

Make a compost pile with your dead leaves or heap them into a big pile and jump in them.

Go to an apple orchard by yourself. Eat apples and drink fresh cider. Walk out into the orchard and shake apples from a tree.

NOVEMBER

Prune and thin your raspberry bushes and then examine the pattern of scratches on your hands and arms.

This is your last chance to plant those spring bulbs.

DECEMBER

Stuff lemons, limes and crab apples into a tall glass or plastic cylinder as a Holiday decoration. Trail ivy in and around it.

Bake Christmas cookies and make candy with your husband, your children, your grandchildren, your friends, your enemies. Love them.

A POCKET FULL OF POSIES

"Mistress Mary,
Quite contrary,
How does your garden grow?
With silver bells,
And cockle shells,
And pretty maids all in a row."

When I learned this nursery rhyme as a three-year old, I envisioned a teen-aged Mistress Mary dressed in a Bo-Peep-type costume looking over her small garden of little blue and pink flowers all of which had the faces of pretty girls. I had no idea what "cockle" or "contrary" meant. I had no idea that Mistress Mary was really Mary, Queen of Scots (1542-1587). She was so hard to get along with that she was banished to the wilds of Scotland where she continued to be so contrary that she ended up with her head severed from her body. When we lived in Edinburgh, our then eight-year old daughter, Kathy, went to a Scottish school where the girls would tie their coats together, put a girl in the middle, toss her in the air and sing lustily, "Mary, Queen of Scots had her head chopped off!" At "chopped off," the girl would be bounced as far as possible into the air.

Some of our nursery rhymes are coded historical anecdotes. The story goes that most of the people in the British Isles were illiterate until relatively recent times. The news of the day, if it was big news, would be sung around the cities and countryside in verse and doggerel. In 1562 these songs were completely comprehensible to all. But to us living 500 years later these verses have become just cute rhymes that we learn and pass on as fit for the nursery crowd.

"Rings on her fingers,
Bells on her toes.

She shall have music
Wherever she goes."

To child-like me this was a woman who was a one-man band. It turns out to be a relic from the Plague Times in the 1500's. Whether or not the great Bubonic Plague which took the lives of one out of every two Europeans was a pestilence sent from God to punish egregious sin, the prostitutes profited from the fact that no one wanted to go into a house where someone was dead of the plague. The bold ladies of easy virtue used to go in and steal from the dead. Clad in purloined rich gowns and jewels, they would attach bells to their shoes to call attention to their stolen finery and their immunity from Divine retribution.

Another very popular rhyme from the Plague Times is:

"Ring around the rosey,
Pocket full of posies.
Ashes, ashes.
We all fall down."

In Ohio we used to all clasp hands and careen around in a circle. At "all fall down," we did. This frolic accurately reflects the fact that even though many carried herbal and floral nosegays thought to ward off the plague, the disease was so relentless that half the population of Europe fell down, returned to the ashes of the earth from whence they came.

"Little Miss Muffet
Sat on a tuffet,
Eating her curds and whey;
Along came a spider,
Who sat down beside her
And frightened Miss Muffet away."

Yes, I thought, a little girl like me sitting on a tuffet, whatever that was. I'm eating curds and whey, whatever that is, and along comes a terrible and big spider and I, like Miss Muffet, leave quickly. No, the

Miss Muffet is Mary Queen of Scots again and the big spider is the reformer John Knox denouncing her from the great pulpit of St. Giles church. Some opine that Miss Muffet was a certain Patience Muffet (or Moffett or Moufet) whose father was a prominent studier of spiders (araneologist) around 1604. By the way, a "tuffet" is a nonsense word, so your imagination can go wild. I prefer a hassock-like pillow covered with lavender satin (to go with her yellow silk skirt and white, puffy-sleeved blouse). And "curds and whey" is cottage cheese as any good dieter knows.

Another queen who inspired a nursery rhyme or two was Queen Anne.

"I am Queen Anne, of whom 'tis said
I'm chiefly famed for being dead.
Queen Anne, Queen Anne, she sits in the sun,
As fair as a lily, as brown as a bun."

Queen Anne (1665-1714) was the last Stuart ruler of England and her reign inspired a certain type of architecture with turrets that still dot the New England town in which I live. The rhyme depicts her as famous for being dead which can be said of most of the people who have ever lived, so she was not particularly effective as a ruler. She did, however, love do to what I and millions like me love to do---watch our gardens. She would sit in her gardens at Kensington with all her ladies in waiting and they waited for the sun to go down as they talked and laughed and got brown as a bun. We may not have as extensive an array of gardens as this queen did. We may not be attended by servants. But we bask in the same sun as queens do and the same flowers warm the cockles of our hearts.

Oh, did my young heart go out to Little Jumping Joan.

"Here am I,
Little Jumping Joan;
When nobody's with me

I'm all alone."

Poor little girl. Jumping up and down, playing all by herself because she was an orphan or she had no friends or something worse. Well, forget poor Joan. "Jumping Joan" was one of the many things they called whores in the 1600's. And their come-on was "when nobody's with me, I'm all alone."

Have you ever taken a course in "Sexual Allusions in Shakespeare?" I have and it's not uplifting. Seems ole Will knew about every word and phrase in the Dictionary of Slang that had anything remotely to do with sex. Since that course, whenever I read "To be or not to be," I think yea, right, what does that really, really mean. That's sort of how I feel about nursery rhymes now.

Take this one.
"Willy, Willy Wilkin,
Kissed the maids a-milking,
Fa, la, la!
And with his merry daffing,
He set them all a-laughing,
Ha, Ha, Ha!"

What does "daffing" really mean? And how about "Fa, la la!" With the exclamation point, no less?

But we shouldn't be suspicious of all nursery rhymes, should we?

"Can you make me a cambrick shirt,
Parsley, sage, rosemary and thyme,
Without any seam or needle work?
And you shall be a true lover of mine."

Here's the Simon and Garfunkel song! Here's Mrs. Robinson! In the old days a man asked a woman to make him a shirt. If she did, that meant he had asked her to marry him and she had accepted. That seems straightforward enough. Nothing suspicious here. But why did they put in "parsley, sage, rosemary and thyme?" Look it up and... Really in the world of nursery

43

rhymes, appearance isn't reality. Those herbs were a refrain from a witch's incantation. Stuck right there in the middle of a marriage proposal!

My grandmother taught me a riddle rhyme when I was very little and even then I knew it was "bad."
"Long, slim and slender;
Tickles where it's tender.
Bald head.
No nose.
Tickles where the hair grows.
What is it?"

She'd laugh, throw her liberated head back and reveal, "It's a buggy whip!" What was a buggy whip, I wondered? What was that other thing, too?

I've always liked to riddle things out. Proverbs 25:2 says, "The glory of God is to conceal a thing." I think this means that the truly interesting truths as well as the Truth must be searched and puzzled out. We are created to prod, probe and push until...boom! There it is!

See if you can unravel this true gardener's riddle:
"As white as milk,
And not milk.
As green as grass,
And not grass.
As red as blood,
And not blood.
As black as soot,
And not soot."

It tastes sweet as honey, but not honey. It's seedy, but not a seed. It can be eaten raw with sugar and milk, baked in a pie or laced in a pudding, grown in the garden or found in the woods. It starts as a white flower, turns into a green thing, then a red thing, then a black thing and we pick it and we get scratched. It's a...blackberry.

But there have to be nursery rhymes that aren't an exercise in etiology. Surely this one:

"Daffy-down-dilly is new come to town,
With a yellow petticoat and a green gown."

Everyone knows that Daffy-down-dilly is a daffodil in the spring with its pretty yellow trumpet and green leaves, don't they? Well, the nursery rhyme book I'm reading right now illustrates Daffy-down-dilly as a young woman dressed in sixteenth century clothes with the wind at her back and her bonnet blowing and she's hurrying down a street lined with houses that look like they belong in Deerfield, Massachusetts. There's not a flower in sight. Obviously, everyone doesn't know.

I guess the thing about nursery rhymes and why we say them and can say them even if we are senile is that they really do mean things other than what they seem to mean. Shakespeare was big on Appearance Versus Reality and he's lasted so long because he was the best at saying something we all could understand and meaning something which only some of us will ever understand. Nursery rhymes have to be the second best at that particular type of verbal artistry.

My favorite is not an English rhyme but an old Persian proverb:

"He who knows and knows not that he knows is asleep. Wake him.

He who knows not and knows not that he knows not is a fool. Shun him.

He who knows not and knows that he knows not is a child. Teach him.

But he who knows and knows that he knows is wise. Follow him."

So when we read those nursery rhymes to our children, when we say them to our grown-up selves, when we mouth them in our wheelchairs in nursing homes, maybe we are knowing that we know not what we are knowing. Maybe we're asleep. Wake us.

GO EAST, YOUNG MAN!

And he did. In the thirteenth century the young Italian, Marco Polo, dazzled Europe with his descriptions of the fabled Orient. His expeditions initiated an East-West cultural exchange that continues to this day.

Marco Polo astonished Italy with the Chinese noodle that the Italians refined for the world as pasta. Yes, the Italians didn't invent spaghetti. (Yes, the Italians did invent pizza---known as far back as 54 B.C.)

But the culinary contributions of the Orient are infinitesimal in comparison to their horticultural migrations. The Peach, Peony and Orange are depicted in Chinese script as far back as 2737 B.C. If China had only given us the workhorse Hostas, that would have been gift enough. But she showered us with the Flowering Almonds, Wisterias, Flowering Crab Apples, Jasmines, Weigelas, Rhododendrons, Azaleas and Pomegranates.

Japan traces its origin to a settlement of Chinese elite and its gardening achievements certainly point to a sophisticated intelligence. That island ceded us the incomparable Day Lilies in 1832 and the symbolic Resurrection Easter Lily in 1819. Many of Japan's gifts sport her name: Japanese Iris, Japanese Maple, Japanese Snowball, Japanese Anemone, Japanese Quince.

Basil, Black Pepper, Nutmeg, Mace, Cinnamon and knobby Ginger found their way from the East to spice our western tables.

The complex Chrysanthemum, however, wins First Prize in Horticultural Exchange. The Occident loves them, builds Shows around them, wears them on lapels and sticks, plants them in their yards, has buckets of them on their porches and in their homes and has hybridized them into spoons, spikes and cacti.

The East has for millennia painted them, written of them, sung to them, studied them and, yes, eaten them. (See the next page for a delicious recipe.)

CHINESE MUM BOWL

For an easy, unusual dinner party or for a fondue-type family moveable feast on late Autumn evenings, try this scrumptious, nutritious CHINESE MUM BOWL-- courtesy of the inscrutable East.

Serves: 4-6

1 lb. chicken breast, skinless, boneless, sliced into bite-sized chunks
1 lb. sirloin of beef, sliced into bite-sized chunks
1/2 lb. medium-large shrimp, shelled
1/2 lb. filet of sole, sliced into bite-sized chunks
1 doz. clams, shucked
Arrange all the above on a pretty platter. Place on the table. Sprinkle with:

Salt and Pepper
2 Tbsps. dry sherry
2 Tbsps. peanut oil
1/2 cup coriander leaves (or parsley), chopped

Boil 8 cups of chicken stock (bouillon) in a fondue bowl in the middle of your table. Add:

1 cup Oriental noodles
1 lb. fresh spinach leaves
1 lb. fresh Chrysanthemum leaves (Can be bought at a Chinese food store.)
2 pieces bean curd, sliced
2 tsps. fresh ginger, grated
When the noodles, leaves and curd are cooked, let each family member or guest spear chunks of meat and seafood with a fondue fork. Dip in the boiling broth and cook to taste.

Serve in medium-sized Chinese bowls (or whatever you have) with some of the broth, leaves, noodles and curd ladled over the meat and seafood. Yum!

THINGS TO DO WITH GINGER ROOT

Since I've mentioned ginger in the last pages, I thought I would suggest a few ways to use ginger. It's one of the oldest known spices. The Greeks and Romans imported this buff-colored root from India. In fact, the Medieval craving for spices like ginger and cinnamon to flavor their bland diet spawned the whole Age of Exploration that culminated in the discovery of America. Columbus was, you remember, seeking a shorter route (The Spice Route) to India.

Ginger was so valuable in the 15th century that a pound of ginger root was worth a whole sheep. Perhaps you've never explored Zingiber officinale. Try these user-friendly ways to spice up your meals.

Get a nice knob of fresh ginger at the store. Peel it. Cut it into 1" pieces. Put the pieces in a wide-mouthed jar (e.g. mayonnaise jar). Fill the jar to the top with a dry Sherry. Seal with a tight-fitting lid. Store in the refrigerator and use the ginger-flavored Sherry to flavor chicken and seafood dishes, desserts, sauces and soups. It stores indefinitely.

For any recipe that calls for fresh ginger, just take out a piece of the ginger from the sherry and use it as you would raw ginger.

A SIMPLE DESSERT USING YOUR GINGER-FLAVORED SHERRY

4 egg yolks
1/3 cup sugar
Dash of salt
2 cups heavy cream, scalded
1/2 cup ginger-flavored Sherry

In a large bowl beat the egg yolks, sugar and salt until the mixture is very light. Add the scalded heavy cream in a steady stream, whisking all the time. Place the custard in a pan and cook it on top of the stove over low heat. Stir constantly with a wooden spoon until the mixture thickens and coats the spoon. Remove from heat. Allow the custard to cool. When cool, stir in the 1/2 cup ginger-flavored Sherry. Pour the custard into custard cups. Chill. Decorate this delicious light dessert with candied flowers or whipped cream.

DIOS de los FLORES

"You tell me then that I must perish
Like the flowers that I cherish.
Nothing remaining of my name,
Nothing remembered of my fame?
But the gardens that I planted still are young---
The songs I sang will still be sung!"

The Aztec poet Huexotzin c. 1484

When Hernando Cortes and four hundred Conquistadors entered the Aztec capital of Tenochtitlan about 500 years ago, the true treasures were not the gold, silver and precious stones they found. The true treasures were the fabled flowers of Montezuma.

Everywhere the young Spaniards looked there were flowers. Official delegations were wreathed in garlands of roses. Aztec businessmen routinely carried bouquets or a single choice flower tied to the end of a stick. Children pelted each other with balls of flowers. Flower gardens proliferated in the town squares, the palace grounds, beside the roads, on the rooftops of all the houses and, miraculously, flowers flourished in the great lake which surrounded the Aztec capital, Tenochtitlan (modern day Mexico City).

These floating gardens, chinampas, were a unique contribution to horticultural technique. The Aztecs cut huge pieces of sod and built mud flower beds whose sides were kept in place by reeds, rushes and other fibrous materials. They launched them onto the great lake. These floating islands were 20 to 300 feet in length and 7 to 40 feet wide. They were firm enough to allow the growth of small willow trees. On the larger gardens the resourceful Aztec often had a small hut where he could siesta after hot mornings of work.

The smaller gardens were simply floated to shore and taken to market when the flowers and vegetables were mature. With a long pole the gardener could change the position of his little piece of earth at will. This floating archipelago of flowers and vegetables undulated and swayed in the lake as far the astonished eye could see.

Cortes was so impressed with these chinampas and the other Aztec gardens that his very first reports to the King of Spain were filled with descriptions of gardens which the palaces of Europe could not hope to rival. He rhapsodized about the Valley of Mexico with its picturesque assemblage of water, woodlands, shining cities, forests of oak, sycamore and cedar and intermingling all were blooming gardens of amaryllis, zinnias, morning glories, convulvus and dahlias---all the gaudy and gorgeous New World flowers whose vibrant colors so influenced the Aztecs' palette.

In the midst of their gardens were pools for bathing and for show. There were tanks of water for exotic fish; orchards of sweet fruits; lattice work from which hung roses, grapes and creepers of all kinds; walkways bordered by roses and flowering shrubs; aviaries; herb gardens for decocting medicines; zoos for exotic animals; carved masonry; cages with reptiles; and innumerable fountains splashing into intricate irrigation canals.

Aztec gardeners were constantly dispatched to other parts of the realm for plants. These trees and shrubs were brought back just like we receive them today with the attached ball of earth wrapped in woven cloth. If there was a plant a nobleman couldn't find, he would have a painting of it made upon his garden wall. So passionate were these Aztecs about flowers that they had a special god for them: Dios de los Flores, God of the Flowers. But Dios de los Flores demanded a lot.

When those intrepid 400 entered Tenochtitlan, its streets and altars stank of and ran with blood. The hundreds (some say thousands) of weekly victims were blood redemption for their lavish lifestyle and their fears. All Aztec gods demanded blood. The priests, nobles, Montezuma and even his household pets ate the thighs and arms of the sacrificed victims.

It is well known that dried blood is one of the most potent fertilizers for a garden. It is a truism that he who lives by the sword dies by the sword.

The seemingly civilized Valley of Flowers was doomed when the first priest thrust his flint knife into the bosom of the first virgin. It was just a matter of Time.

But there were flowers amidst all the blood!

There always are.

For further exploration of the gardens of the Aztecs:
The Conquest of Mexico by William Prescott
The Conquest of New Spain, an eyewitness account by one of the Conquistadors Bernal Diaz

JOHNNY'S SO LATE AT THE FAIR

"Oh, dear, what can the matter be?
Dear, dear, what can the matter be?
Oh, dear, what can the matter be?
Johnny's so late at the fair."
The O.E.D. defines a "fair" as "a periodical gathering of buyers and sellers." The State Fairs of today are the survivors of a long tradition of get-togethers that go way back to the Middle Ages. The fairs of the Middle Ages usually opened on an important church holiday. The cathedral bells pealed, banners hung from the city buildings and there were no rooms at the inns. People came from all around for the great St. Bartholomew Fair in Smithfield outside of London. Jugglers and acrobats and puppeteers and merchants and food mongers set up stages and stalls in the town. Merchants would travel all the way to India or Russia just to get spices, silks, amber and furs to sell during Fair days. The serfs and nobles of medieval society flocked to these gatherings of commerce, entertainment and food.

The first State Fair in the United States was an agricultural fair in Pittsfield, Massachusetts in 1810. Its purpose was to give the farmers a place to display their livestock and the vegetables and flowers from their gardens. Prizes were awarded for the largest pumpkin, the best rooster, the most perfect rose, etc. Entertainment was offered as a way to pay for the prizes. The farmers loved getting together and learning about new farming methods. Their families loved the excitement of the week-long respite from rural life.

New York state appropriated money for a state fair in 1819 and other states soon followed. Soon every state had a Fairgrounds with permanent buildings for the livestock, halls for the fruits of harvest and an amphitheater for races and entertainments.

Every September my husband Steve and I took our three children to the Danbury State Fair in Connecticut. The older two, Kathy and Blake, were allowed to skip school for this all-day festival into the world of farm animals, feats of oxen strength, lumberjack agility, Ferris wheels and hucksters touting the latest food gadgets and home furnishings.

There were always interesting sideshows: the largest lobster ever caught in American waters--a dead monster umpteen feet long housed in its own gypsy caravan. We'd pay the dollar, go into the darkened wagon and wonder at that humongous red crustacean mounted on the wall beside its master who told us three or four unbelievable things then hurried us out the other door.

A man with performing chimpanzees had a small amphitheater near Frontier Village. He was a bored, seedy man whose life had obviously taken an unexpected turn. We suspected him of abusing the chimps and wondered whether we should call the A.S.P.C.A.

I always headed for the huge Bingo Hall where regulars played ten cards at a time. I was a once-a-year Bingoist who pawed through the frayed cards looking for a good one. Steve took our little Jesse for rides on the dizzying toy airplanes that he both feared and hated as I hopefully placed kernels of corn on B-10 and G-52. I was out-kerneled every time by the pros.

Steve went to the Danbury Fair for two reasons: the food and the food. When we entered the iron gates, he headed for the messy food, the food that tasted good but was a bear to eat: buns with unwieldy sausages smothered in onions and peppers and a brothy sauce; hard strips of beef covered with shredded lettuce and a yogurt dill sauce that leaked out over his fingers and onto his shirt.

We all loved the hot fried dough sprinkled with powdered sugar. Usually we ended up eating lunch in one of the huge tents where turkey, gravy, mashed potatoes, pork, sauerkraut and baked ham were served on too thin paper plates with flimsy plastic forks and knives.

For our family the rides were not the big attraction at the state fair. We preferred to sit in the bleachers and watch farmers urge truculent oxen to pull tons of dead weight cement across a finish line. We talked about how the men and animals must have practiced so hard all year for this moment of glory. We wondered at the different ways people choose to lead their lives.

Our favorite attraction, and we had to line up and wait for this one, was the Swedish Sven and his son, Tom, who were experts at sawing wood in half in record time. They had souped-up saws and competed against each other. The father was a giant of a man who won most of the time. The son was big and had youth on his side, but Sven had experience. We'd imagine their lives and wonder how in the world they ever decided to become the Sawing Wonders. They have over the years become part of our family's lore and discussions. They probably would be amazed to know that.

We always ended up watching for an hour or two the man who cut fruit and vegetables with that gadget that worked perfectly for him but wouldn't work for you when you bought it and brought it home. Every year, even after we had bought it and knew it didn't really work that way for normal people, every year we hung at the back of his semi-circle and were mesmerized by his skill and spiel.

A woman, the same woman, was always there in the Home Section. She was from Pennsylvania and demonstrated her steel butterfly mold. She'd dip this winged pattern into batter and transfer it to hot oil. Seconds later, it was brought out of the oil and the butterfly slipped perfectly off the mold and onto a paper towel. She would sprinkle these perfect beauties with some powdered sugar and offer all of us a taste. They were wonderful! For several years I watched her. One year I just had to have that gadget. I bought it. I heated up the oil. I dipped the steel butterfly into the batter. I plopped it into the hot oil. It broke into a hundred sizzling bits of fried batter. The rest clung to the steel mold and later resisted all efforts to remove it. The following year I told her my experience. She said the oil wasn't hot enough and the mold wasn't tempered.

In the early evening when the September sun had sunk low behind the Great Hall, we would all meet at the entrance gate and walk so far to our car. Kathy and Blake had a trinket or two that they had won throwing balls at bottles or shooting targets. Jesse was tired and Steve carried him on his shoulders. We were filthy dirty and full of fair food. By the time we got out of the parking lot, the lights were on in the Fairgrounds. We could hear the squeals from the rides and see the huge Ferris wheel churning against the black sky. We didn't talk much on the ride back home. Jesse usually fell asleep.

Nothing was the matter.

We had just been so late at the Fair.

HOW I GOT MY BEES

The year before the Danbury Fair closed in 1981 there was a special exhibit that they hadn't had before. It was a small, 6 ft. by 6 ft., enclosed room which promised thousands of bees. Nobody but me wanted to go in. The man charged two dollars. I paid my money and entered. It was very dark inside. When my eyes became accustomed, I found myself surrounded on all four sides by hundreds of thousands of honeybees behind glass. It was a glass room filled with multiple hives.

At first I was overwhelmed by so many bees and a bit frightened. But I went up to the glass and started looking at them. Millions, maybe, of tiny life forms were there where they couldn't hurt me and I could see them carrying on with their lives. Within fifteen minutes I knew I wanted to have something like this for myself.

I had NEVER been interested in bees. They were always something to stay away from. They could hurt you. So this wasn't an evolutionary interest which culminated in that experience. The experience I had in that little, dark glass room at the Danbury Fair was apocalyptic in the true sense of that word: "the veil was drawn away" from something and revealed to me something which I had never thought about before.

I stayed in the room about an hour. The man who kept the bees talked to me about them. I asked him if there was any way that I could have something like that for myself, for my own observation. He told me there were observation hives. These were small hives with a glass panel that allowed one to view the life of the bees. He said I would have to find a beekeeper in my neighborhood. He could probably order me such a hive and get me a package of bees.

Sandra Sweeny Silver

I told Steve that I wanted to do this. He was adamant that I would not. He was very afraid of bees and had once carried a bee which he thought was a killer bee (prematurely arrived in Connecticut) around in a vial in his car for one year. The bee was a victim of one of his raids on a nest outside our front door. He thought it was so big and so mean that someone at the University of Connecticut extension in Stamford should look at it and confirm the fact that it was a killer. I don't know what happened to that bee, but he never had it examined. Nevertheless, he was not in favor of the idea nor was my son Blake who detested bees, too. He was a partner in that early morning raid on the nest. They had both risked their lives to destroy those bees.

But I was going to have my bees. I knew they weren't going to get out and hurt us. The man had assured me it was a very safe hobby.

There wasn't anything under BEES in the telephone directory. But I did see an article in our local newspaper about a man who was going to give a lecture on honeybees at the library in Wilton. I contacted him. That's how Ed Weiss and the honeybees came into my life.

Ed and his wife, Nita, have a home on a bumpy old road in Wilton, Connecticut. Nita has some of the nicest flower gardens I've ever seen. "It's the bees," she says. Behind their house they have about 60 hives that stand behind the gardens and stumble almost into the woods. Ed is always busy. He has converted his garage into a honey production center and his brownish thick honey sells in local stores under the label Wilton Gold. He always talks about how he quit the high corporate world to raise honeybees. I told him I wanted an observation hive. He said it could be done. I ordered one for delivery with a package of bees in April of 1982.

In preparation for our new experience, Steve and I went to Ed's for a demonstration of hiving. There were about 20 people there. They all were getting outdoor hives. My hiving would be different, would be one which I would have to follow by the book that came with my hive. But Steve and I stood there in the circle that surrounded Ed as he poured out 10,000 bees onto a white sheet. We watched them make a beeline into the hive which he had prepared. Steve had tucked his pants into his boots. He had zipped his leather jacket up under his chin and his hands were in his pockets. He thought all the other people were weird types and tried to figure out how I fit into all this.

But we both observed that no one was stung, that the bees seemed intent on entering rather than on stinging. We felt better. He had seen that I would not be deterred and had resigned himself to the situation as one does in a marriage. He was there at the hiving because I had told him he had to help me, that I couldn't hive them by myself. I loved him very much on that cold March morning.

And then I got my bees. And then we all got bees. And then we were all amazed and pleasantly so as one is when someone arrives to stay who turns out to be fascinating and independent and giving.

THE SLAUGHTER OF THE DRONES

"The Slaughter of the Drones." Sounds like a Machiavellian solution to worker apathy. In fact, it is just one of the many iterations in the life of the honeybee hive.

The hive of the honeybee (apis mellifera) is composed of one queen, many female workers and a scattering of males called drones. The queen lays the eggs and is, for all intents and purposes, a prisoner in her own castle. The female workers do all the work in the hive and all the foraging and gathering outside the hive.

The male drones do...well, the drones do very little. They don't clean the hive or take care of developing brood or gather nectar, pollen, propolis or water. I have seen their large, furry selves obsequiously begging a female for a little nectar. She stops, gives him from her nectar crop and then hurries on to her busy life as he continues to meander over the honeycomb sipping here and there from the golden hexagons.

His life begins like hers in the Spring. She is born and bred to work. He is born and bred, as far as we can determine, to fertilize the queen.

One fine Spring day when the sun is blazing and the earth is pregnant with bloom, the virgin queen pokes her head outside the hive entrance. She lifts her sleek, long body into the clear air and begins to climb toward the sun. Drones from her hive and the other hives nearby smell her scent and begin to follow her. Only one drone will catch this pristine beauty. She is bigger than they and faster than most. Up, up she flies...so high the mating itself has never been observed though some old beekeepers have claimed to hear a crack at consummation.

The many drones with their powerful bodies wing toward her in a tangled comet-like horde. The fastest, most powerful catches her in mid-flight. As he impregnates her for life, part of his abdomen tears off inside her to plug his seed. He falls lifeless to the sane earth. His genes will live on for generations. His death was worth it.

The mated queen returns to the hive, begins laying eggs and never again leaves the hive unless the bees swarm. The other drones return to their hives and their rather sybaritic life of eating, flying around and heavy buzzing until...

One fine Autumn day when the sun is waning, the nights are cold and the flowers are few, they return to the hive and the female guard bees refuse to let them enter...too many unproductive mouths to feed over the long, cold winter ahead. Those females who tended them as larvae, fed them as adults and lived peacefully side by cramped side with them for a summer lifetime now bar them from the warm hive so that they will freeze to death in the cold, fallen nights.

On crunchy, crisp October mornings I have seen them dead in the stones and grass outside the window where my observation hive is. They haven't "slaughtered" them all. I can see a few drones inside the hive creeping close to the winter cluster. But the majority of the males are gone.

A few are allowed to live. One never knows when a queen will die and a new virgin will need to be mated.

There are no parallels to be drawn to human existence, no points to be made by smug feminists. Each---the queen, the worker and the drone---has glory and gaffe. The queen, a lonely focal point, imprisoned by her subjects and her fecundity. The worker, anonymous and servile, paradigm of sacrifice and productivity. And the drone, virile and magnificent, sine qua non, driven to a doomed consummation, slaughtered by his daughters.

HONEY AND THE HONEYBEE

"My son, eat thou honey because it is good: and the honeycomb which is sweet to the taste. So shall the knowledge of wisdom be to thy soul."

When King Solomon penned this proverb (Proverbs 24:13) 3,000 years ago, man had already domesticated Apis mellifera, the honeybee. Two thousand years before Solomon even lived, the ancient Egyptians in c. 2800 B.C. floated apiaries (many beehives) on barges up and down the Nile. The honeybees would fly from flower to flower on the narrow strip of cultivated land on either side of the Nile River. When the hives were full of honey, the ancients would brave the stings and get the liquid gold for trade with the Middle and Far East.

Honey was literally worth its weight in gold thousands of years ago. Why? Because it has been man's ONLY sweetener for most of his history. And we really have a sweet tooth. When the sugar cane was introduced into Europe in the 1200's, it was called "the honeyed reed" because we had no reference for "sweet" other than "honey." The honeybee is THE ONLY WAY the sugars found in the nectar from flowers can be collected and transformed into honey.

Honey is one of the honeybees' main foods. She, for the foragers of nectar are all women, needs honey for her own existence and for the existence of all members of her hive. When she forages, she collects three things: nectar to be transformed into honey, pollen for food and for the developing brood and propolis which is a miraculous substance found on blossoms and acts as an antibiotic in the hive and as a glue for hive repairs.

In addition to being the honeybees' main food, honey has become a standard for people the world over. Its curative powers have been touted and largely unchallenged for millennia. Listen to this. Just one spoonful of honey contains: water; 7 kinds of sugars including dextrose, levulose and sucrose; 12 kinds of acids including amino, citric, formic and acetic; numerous minerals including calcium, sodium phosphorus, potassium, sulfur, magnesium, iron, copper, manganese, silica, silicon, chloride; proteins; vitamins including thiamine, riboflavin, ascorbic acid, pentothenic acid, Vitamin K and biotin; enzymes including phospatase, diastase, invertase and catalase; terpenes; aldehydes; acetylcholine; some propolis; some pollen and some wax both of which contain vitamins, minerals, acids, enzymes, etc. Little wonder beekeepers boast more centenarians than any other profession on the face of the earth! One spoonful of raw honey a day keeps a lot at bay.

But the most amazing thing to me about honey is not that so much is packed into so little. The amazing thing is the tenacity and bravery that the little honeybee exhibits as she collects the nectar for her honey. A typical foraging honeybee visits 30,000 flowers a day! She has a nectar crop in which the nectar is stored. She inserts her proboscis (nectar tongue) into the womb of the flower, withdraws the nectar and places it in her nectar crop, visits another bloom and another, returns to the hive, disgorges the nectar into a hexagonal cell and then flies out again and again and again. Her life span is only about 6 weeks and several weeks of that time are spent foraging.

I have seen an "old" forager's wings. Tattered and torn and threadbare are these gossamer glories which wing her to her duty. She can pierce through the air at speeds up to 18 mph and battle 15 mph winds laden with nectar which weighs as much as she does! She literally dies working or carrying home one more load for the hive.

Most have working hives that are placed in their yards or fields, but I have a laboratory hive in my kitchen window with a glass panel for observation. One spring I had to break into my observation hive because all the bees in my hive had died over the winter from a bee disease.

In order to hive new healthy bees, I had to break the glass, scoop out the dead bees, clean out (with a special tool called a hive tool) all the incredible mess along the walls and floor of the hive, install new comb and then have the glass company come over and measure for a new glass front. It is a hard and sticky job to break into a dead hive and prepare it for new bees! It usually takes me about sixteen hours. I always leave the old combs out by my bed of thyme so that the honeybees can pick them clean. Maybe some of their relatives made that honey. But that year, the honey in the hive was white! I kept that honey for myself and gently heated off the wax.

For honey is not always honey-colored. Sweet clover honey has a greenish tinge. There is a honey produced in North Carolina that is bluish. The exact nectar source for that honey is unknown. Pink honey is found in parts of California. Acacia, citrus, ilex, sage and raspberry honeys are white. The white honey in my hive must have come from the many raspberry bushes on my property. It tasted like honey, but it was lighter. Not only the color but the consistency and taste of honey all depend on the primary source of nectar for the honeybee.

One pint of honey weighs one and a half pounds. A whole colony of honeybees has to make 37,000 trips to the fields to produce just one pound of honey. So for that little one-pint jar of honey you get in the supermarket, the honeybees had to make about 55,500 flights to the fields and back again.

As you spoon that liquid gold onto your hot biscuit, be grateful to the little honeybee.

Nectar is converted to honey by the action of the bee's salivary juices and by the evaporation of water from the nectar in the hive. Its actual conversion from nectar to honey contains many unknowns, but that is the essence.

Right now as you are reading these words, millions of honeybees are hatching in wild and domesticated hives all over America. And millions of honeybees are foraging the tiny blossoms in yards and fields gathering the precious fluid to make honey. Inside the hive night and day the queen bee is laying eggs that will turn into bees to replace the old foragers. They, in turn, will feed and tend the larvae and work the fields until in six weeks, they are replaced by another generation of honeybees who will tend and forage and be replaced. Their life cycle is short compared to ours. Their work schedule is more rigorous and their time for play is nil.

But I like to think that as they are producing the 226 million pounds of honey we consume each year in America that they love what they do. Imagine being created to bury your body tens of thousands of times each day in the tender tendrils of the sweet clover or the waxy petals of the hidden ilex flowers or the high crowns of the oak blooms or the low jewels of the ajuga! Imagine venturing into the bowels of a flower and plundering the very essence of life's liquid! Imagine seeing every thing with 34,000 facets per eye each with its own lens! Imagine the beauty, the majesty, the mosaic!

Don't pity the humble honeybee. Only in the Kingdom will you and I glimpse such glory.

HONEY MADE FROM THESE NECTAR SOURCES ARE:

LEGENDARY: The honey made 2,000 years ago from the wild thyme that grew on Mt. Hymettus in Greece.

UNSURPASSED: Wild raspberry.

SUPERB: Acacia, alfalfa, apple, blackberry, campanula, cherry, all citrus, clematis, clovers, fireweed, ilex, heaths, heathers, locust, logwood, manzanita, pea family, peach, pear, sage, sumac, thyme, sourgum, willow-herb.

GOOD: Asparagus, basswood, black mangrove, blueberry, button bush, cabbage palmetto, Canada thistle, cascara Sagrada, cotton, dandelion, date palm, eucalyptus, gourd family, guava, heartsease, horehound, horsemint, maple, mesquite, mints, mistletoe, moca, onion family, paloverde, pepper tree, phacelia, royal palm, saw palmetto, sourwood tree, soy bean, Spanish needle, sunflower, sweet pepper bush, thistle, tobacco, tulip or yellow poplar.

POOR: Ailanthus, aster, buckwheat, cactus, chinquapin, cowpea, goldenrod, partridge pea.

POSSIBLY POISONOUS: Azalea, black nightshade, California buckeye, death camas, dodder, honey-dew collected from the New Zealand leafhopper, ironwood tree, jessamine, locoweed, mountain laurel, rhododendron, tutu tree in Australia.

NOTE: Most supermarket honeys are a mixture of various nectars. The clovers are the honeybees' primary nectar source. The best honey for you is RAW honey which doesn't look as pretty but has not been heated. The above honeys are graded assuming the nectar is collected ALMOST EXCLUSIVELY from these plants. That rarely happens because the honeybee forages in a three-mile radius. The possibility of being actually poisoned from honey consumption is almost zero. There was a famous case thousands of years ago when an army in the Peloponessian War raided a wild hive and hundreds of them died. I gave honey and water to all of my children when they were infants and they thrived on it.

APPLE CAKE SAUCED WITH WARM CARAMEL

Apple blossoms are beloved by artists and bees. In the Spring the honeybee wings her way to the apple trees in our yard, sticks her little nectar tongue in the center of that pink-white beauty and quaffs to her heart's delight. If pollen is the seed of nature, nectar is its drink. You can eat these blossoms. All fruit tree blossoms have a soft, faintly sweet taste.

In the Spring these flowers (which will become apples after the bees cross pollinate them) can be used to decorate a cake. Just plop several of them on top of the icing or tuck a twig of them on the plate beside the cake.

As I type the heading of this recipe, my mouth waters. What's a better taste than a spicy apple cake with gooey caramel dripping from it? My mother baked the best spice cake iced with caramel frosting! I'd come home from school and there would be only one piece missing from the cake. She had cut a square of that good cake for herself while it was still warm. She had poured herself a cup of fresh black coffee, gone into the sunroom, opened a book on Epictetus and enjoyed the fruits of her labor. Thank you, Mother, for all the considerate baking you did, for your constant presence when I came in the door and yelled for you, for the home you and Dad built for me, for the values you instilled in me, for how much of yourself you gave to me when you could have given it elsewhere. Thank you.

I'm so glad, Readers, that I had a chance to thank my mother for all this and more while she was still alive. Have you thanked the ones who gave to you so you could have something to give to others? Thank them now. Give them their flowers when they can smell them.

Here's that good recipe.

Serves: 12.

Preheat oven to 350 degrees.
Butter and flour a 13" by 9" by 2" metal baking pan.

2 cups sugar
1/2 cup plus 2 Tbsps. butter, room temperature
2 large eggs
2 tsps. vanilla
2 cups flour
2 tsps. cinnamon
1 tsp. baking soda
1 tsp. baking powder
1/2 tsp. salt
2 lbs. Golden Delicious apples, peeled, cored, coarsely grated
Optional: 1 cup walnuts, chopped

Using an electric beater, beat the sugar, butter, eggs and vanilla in a large bowl until smooth.
Add the flour, cinnamon, baking soda, baking powder and salt. Blend well.
With a spatula stir in the apples and walnuts. Blend well.
Pour the batter into the baking pan. Bake until the top browns and a toothpick inserted into the middle comes out clean (about 55 minutes). Cool in the pan.

To Serve: For the Caramel Sauce, you can make your own favorite recipe or use Mrs. Richardson's Carmel Sauce from the supermarket. Heat the Caramel Sauce until just warm. Cut the cake into squares and dribble the warm Caramel over it.

Note: Invite a friend over to enjoy your cake.

APOCALYPSE SCENARIO

Nowadays Americans are trying to lose weight, cut down on salt and fat, reduce calories and cholesterol, do something about their CRP, exercise, think thin, stay thin.

It's hard for our rich culture to realize that most of the people living today and most of the people who have ever lived have tried to keep weight on, find enough food to eat, increase calories, have thought food, have thought "find food."

Diogenes, the ancient Athenian who went about with a lantern looking for an honest man, was once asked, "When should a man eat?"

He replied.

"If he's a rich man, whenever he wants.

If he's a poor man, whenever he can."

Most of the world eats whenever and whatever it can.

We have been foragers for most of our existence. We have gathered, caught and prepared what grew or moved around us. We took seeds from those plants we liked, planted them and grew them in patches near our shelters. Some believe that the first sign of a civilized society is when it plants seeds in the ground and stays around to harvest them.

But we don't have to go all the way back to pre-history or sub-Sahara Africa to see man foraging for food. Here in America almost 400 years ago very civilized Europeans began settling a virgin land in New England. One out of every two of those civilized Pilgrims starved to death on the shores of Massachusetts because they did not know there was an abundance of edible food around them. The "savage" Squanto and his tribe gave the civilized Europeans a lesson in foraging for food and they survived very well after that.

Even in the dead of winter the Pilgrims could have made bark bread. This was a staple of the Indians when they traveled.

Here's how to make bark bread: Peel away the hard outer bark of the tree and expose the inner cambium layer. You can either chew the sappy wood or dry it in the sun as the Indians did. Sprinkle a little water on the sun-dried bread to revive it and eat. How many people have been found starved to death propped up against a tree? That tree could have saved their lives.

I've often wondered what would happen to a civilized state here in America if a man-made or natural disaster of great proportion hit us. How many of us would starve to death in the midst of plenty as did our Pilgrim forefathers?

Let me build an artificial scenario. Let's say you have a one-acre home in Connecticut. You have some trees, grass, maybe a stream. You have to live for the entire month of APRIL on just what you can forage from your own acre. Could you survive? Could you keep yourself and your whole family alive on just what your land produces?

Let's start foraging.

You have an endless supply of what you try every year to eradicate--Dandelions. They are some of the best tasting and most nutritious of all wild foods. You can literally eat the whole plant. The jagged leaves are, of course, known as a great green. You can eat them raw, put them in a salad, or boil them like the Italians do. I like them raw with some wild onions (bulbs and spikes) and a good bacon dressing. Of course, you can't have that particular dressing unless you have a pig. You will have to kill and dress it and then you will have to smoke the bacon. Do you even know from what part of the pig the bacon comes?

The Dandelion buds can be eaten like capers. The flowers can be depetaled and used as garnish. (I doubt if you'll be "garnishing.") The roots can be dried, ground and boiled in water for a tea. When the early colonists refused to pay the British Tea Tax and had their party there in Boston, their morning, afternoon and evening tea stopped. Englishmen without their tea?! What to do? They gathered the roots of dandelions, dried them and then boiled them in water for their daily Tea Parties. That'll show King George.

Better than lettuce any day are violet leaves--my favorite. There are tens of thousands of these wild delicacies in April in your yard. Gather the leaves and the flowers and use them as a wonderful salad with a vinaigrette. If you don't have any vinaigrette left, just eat these sweet leaves raw. The flowers can be used to decorate cakes, too, but I doubt you'll be baking a lot.

For my taste, the best wild food is the fiddlehead. These are the tiny or fat curled-up frond of the fern itself. In May Maine's main export are fiddleheads. All fronds are edible. Take away the hairy sheath, boil several times and throw off the water until it runs clear. Fiddleheads taste like asparagus, artichokes or green beans. Delicious. The Ostrich fern is the fat, good one.

There are lots of good mushrooms in April: morels, chanterelles, oyster, meadow and shaggy manes. You have to know which are edible and which are poisonous, however. As you know, these can be eaten raw or boiled---take some water from your stream. Put the mushrooms in a bark bowl, or a bowl you've made out of sun-baked mud or in one of your pans if you have any left. Make a fire using either flint or matches (do you have any matches?). Boil the mushrooms just like you used to do before the holocaust.

Your acre is teeming with wild greens most of which you despised---before.

There's mullein, sorrel, tansy, miner's lettuce, purslane, coltsfoot, dock, milkweed, primroses. These are all laden with minerals and Vitamin A. Those tall stinging nettles are growing in April. They're edible. Don't forget to boil off most wild greens until the water is clear.

If you crave a sweet, follow the foraging honeybee back to her wild hive. Brave the stings (they're good for you) and raid their stock. Don't forget to eat the pollen in the hive. It's packed with nutrients. And gather that sticky bee gum, propolis, while you're raiding the hive for the sweet honeycomb. Propolis is an antibiotic. You may need an antibiotic. For another sweet treat, tap one of your maple trees for some remnants of the sweet sap. Don't know how to tap a maple tree? So much to learn.

I love the tiger lilies that grow wild beside the road and in our gardens. They are delicious. In April the shoots are young and tender. Gather them for your wild salad. For something more filling: dig up the fleshy tubers of the day lilies and eat them. Don't forget to eat the wonderful little bulbils clinging to the tubers. If you have some butter and salt and pepper, you'll really have a feast.

Every little thing is important when what you can forage is all you can eat. Later on you can eat the day lily flowers---truly sweet and delicate. If your life were normal, you could stuff the flowers with chicken salad or crabmeat for a stunning and good lunch. Before the flower blooms, you can saute the buds. When the flower is spent, use it to thicken one of your wild sauces or soups. Those little bulbils will be great in that squirrel stew you're preparing.

Squirrels are great wild food. (As with all wild animals, you have to remove certain glands before eating them. I'll tell you about this in the following pages. You don't want to be poisoned!) The original Brunswick Stew is made with squirrel meat.

Catch the rabbits that wander onto your property. Don't forget all the small birds are fresh game. The eggs in their nests make good omelets. Fashion lethal weapons. Fell a deer and roast it over your fire.

None of this is easy!

It's great to be a vegetarian IF you live in America. We have wonderful produce and fruits and tofus and grains right down the street at the market.

BUT, I can tell you this, if you really had to live off the land, sooner rather than later you'd want meat. And you would want to extract and beat the blood from that animal. Americans are the only people in the world who don't eat blood in puddings and sausages even though we all came from countries and peoples who ate blood.

When the Eskimo kills his first walrus or bear in the late winter, he withdraws his spear and stoops to drink the blood. It's the first fresh food he's had all winter long.

As long as you are revolted, don't forget about the most plentiful supply of protein on the planet---insects. Your acre is teeming with insects--ants, grasshoppers, beetles, crickets, cicadas, bees, etc. A tribe in Africa exists solely on roasted grasshoppers. Insects are 50-60% protein versus beef which is only 17% protein. NASA is doing experiments on whether water fleas can be used as a source of protein on long stellar flights.

When an April shower comes along and flushes out all the earthworms, rejoice. They are delicious eating, are 60% protein and only need a little frying. In your stream you probably have some fish, some crayfish, some frogs, minnows. Make a trap or fashion a fishing rod, line and hook. It will try your patience---and luck.

If you want a change of diet, although as you can see, there is plenty of variety--you can eat moss, lichen, liverworts. God often uses these fungi to color parts of the earth where nothing else will grow. The finest display of lichen is on Kerguelen's Island in sub-Antarctica. But you're in Connecticut and your moss is good. The white pine moss is especially nourishing.

If you can take a day or two's hike to the ocean (remember when you could drive?), you can gather the moss that grows on the seashore and on the rocks. Plus you can eat the endless supply of seaweed and algae either raw, sun-dried, boiled or steamed with the clams you've dug up on the sandy shore.

I could go on and on, but I think you see you could not only live but be relatively healthy on the food just on your acre.

Now you would be MUCH thinner. It takes me about 60 minutes to gather enough violets for a violet salad for 5-6 people. That's one hour just for a little, not-very-filling, side salad.

You're on your hands and knees. You're up and down. You're digging and pulling. You're trying to find and then catch a little frog or a squirrel or some earthworms. You're gathering wood for fires and trying to get them going and trying to find things to put food in and things to eat it with and when you're all finished, about six hours later, you've eaten a salad and a piece of meat.

It takes all day every day to forage for food for one decent meal.

Only very recently has a small percentage of us on the planet had the privilege and luxury of saying, "I'm on a diet."

The vast majority of us has always said, "I'm hungry. Let's go find food."

CAUTION: IDENTIFY AS EDIBLE ANY WILD FOOD BEFORE EATING IT

SOME WILD FOODS TO GATHER, COOK, PURSUE

Prickly Pears

The Aztecs, migrating to Mexico from North America (c. 1000-1300 A.D.), saw an eagle atop a prickly pear tree. They saw this as a sign that they were to settle there. That place they called Tenochtitlan. Today it is Mexico City.

You can get prickly pears in most markets. It has a mild, sweet flavor and is usually eaten raw. The thorns hurt, so it is advisable to wear gloves when preparing. Dig out the pointy, black eyes and thorns with a knife or potato peeler. Peel and slice the cactus. Chill. Serve with lemon juice and sugar.

Milkweed (Spring food)

With most wild greens, there is bitterness. To avoid this, boil the wild green in water. Pour off the water and repeat the process three/four times. The final boil is in water with a dash of salt. The young pods are the most interesting part of this ubiquitous plant. Continually boil off the pods. Then you can eat them like broccoli or make an au gratin sauce and bake them for about 25 minutes. The flowers can be cut up and stewed. The leaves can be boiled off and used as greens as can the early spring shoots.

Mullein

Mullein is that very tall, velvety-leafed and yellow-flowered stalk that, defying all logic, will grow through a tiny crack in your cement to stately heights! The leaves can be repeatedly boiled and eaten as a green. It has been used medicinally for catarrh and dysentery. Hummingbirds often collect the hairs on the droopy, fat leaves to line their teeny nests. The Greeks soaked its leaves in oil and used them as wicks for their lamps. The Romans dipped the whole dried stalk in liquid suet to burn as candles for their night processions.

Burdock

This weed is one of the biggest pests in the yard or garden. Its roots are almost impossible to totally eradicate. It intrudes everywhere and in the Fall it grows burrs that hitchhike on you and your children and pets. This is one weed Europe introduced to the New World. We brought dock over from Europe because--we liked it so much we couldn't live without it. (!?) It is an edible and very good-tasting green, however. When boiling it, always use at least two changes of water to remove the tough fibers and the bitterness. In the early Spring, gather the young leaves and use them in salads. The stalk can be eaten raw or boiled. Even those "all-the-way-to-China" taproots are edible. Dig down as far as you want to. Break off the root. Sit down and munch on it as you rest from your labor.

Cattails

We've all waded into swamps and wet places for these brown beauties. Now you can look on them as a source of food as well as decoration. The sprouts, shoots and buds can be used fresh as a vegetable or in salads. The pollen of the cattail can be assiduously gathered and used for baking flour in your wild breads. If you have to eat wild, you can even eat the seeds after the plant has gone to down. Also, save that down for your pillows and poofs.

Carnation Petal Cake

Bake any white or yellow cake you fancy. Cool and ice it. Sprinkle washed and drained carnation petals over the top of the cake. Keep in the refrigerator until tea time.

Wild Salad

To a salad of wild strawberry leaves and violet leaves, add crescents of unpeeled apples. A good vinaigrette is essential. Throw in some of the tiny fraises des bois (wild strawberries), too.

Rose Petal Preserves

This unusual-tasting jam can be used on cakes as well as on breads and rolls.

1 lb. fresh, non-sprayed rose petals
2 lbs. sugar
Juice of one large lemon

Use a stone crock. Alternate a layer of petals with a layer of sugar until you have exhausted your supplies. Finish with a layer of sugar. Then add enough boiling water to cover the rose petals and sugar. Cover the crock with a damp cloth/towel for three days.

At the end of three days, put 1 lb. of sugar and enough water to dissolve it in a big pot. Cook the syrup until a little dropped in cold water forms a soft ball. Add the rose petals and juices to the syrup. Simmer until it gets thick like honey. Remove from heat and stir in the lemon juice. Pour into hot sterilized jam jars and seal with lids or paraffin.

Wild Meats

Possum (Or Beaver, Raccoon, Hedgehog, Etc.)

This strange-looking animal comes out at night and is found mainly in the southern and eastern US. When you catch him, he will pretend to be dead. That is the origin of the expression "Plays possum." The South is famous for Possum Stew and Possum and Sweet Potatoes.

First of all---catch the possum. Skin and clean him. ("Cleaning" means eviscerating, etc.) * Be sure to remove carefully the four waxy-looking little pear-shaped glands. There are two in the small of the back and one each under the forelegs. These are poisonous and MUST be removed. (On some small game animals, there is one each under the hind legs.) After skinning, cleaning and removing the glands, simmer the animal in water for about 30 minutes with some peppers, salt and pepper. Drain. Roast the possum in some of its water for one hour. Thirty minutes into the roasting, put in some peeled and cooked sweet potatoes. Serve in bark bowls.

NOTE: Most of these more exotic game foods (esp. raccoons) taste better if they are aged for a week or so in the snow or in a freezer.

How To Cook If You Don't Have A Stove

Dig a hole about three feet into the earth. Line it with stones. Build a fire in the pit and let it burn for several hours to heat up the stones. When your "oven" is hot, dig out some of the coals and ashes. Put the meat in. It's all right if it gets ashy. Can't stand the ashes? Wrap the meat in a piece of cloth or in heavy leaves or brush.

If you are lucky enough to have some vegetables, put them on top of your meat. Put some of the coals on top of it all. Cover with dirt very tightly so no heat escapes. Allow about 45 minutes per lb. of meat. Don't open the oven until you are ready to eat it, because once opened, your heat is gone. You can bake bread this way, too. They still use this method in parts of Africa and Asia.

To boil something: Just heat up the stones and then take the hot stones and drop them in water. It will make the water boil. Add burdock, vegetables, meat, etc.

Spring Edibles

amaranth, asparagus, bracken and other fern heads, burdock, cattails, chickweed, chicory, chives, dandelions, day lily, dock, elderberry flowers, garlic, henbit, lamb's quarters, leek, milkweed, mint, mulberry, meadow mushrooms, mustard, wild onion, pepper grass, plantain leaves, pokeweed, prickly pear pods, purslane, sassafras, sow thistle, spring beauty, violet, watercress, wild ginger, wild rose, wild strawberry, winter cress, wood sorrel, yucca.

Summer Edibles

bee balm, amaranth, blackberry, black cherry, black raspberry, blueberry, dittany, elderberries, grape, ground cherry, huckleberry, may apple, maypop, papan, plantain, sorrel, sumac, sweet goldenrod, wild plum, wild rice, wild rose hips, burdock, cattails, chickweed, chicory, chives, dandelions, day lily, garlic, lamb's quarters, leek, milkweed, mint, mulberry, meadow mushrooms, mustard, onion, prickly pear pods, purslane, sassafras, sow thistle, spring beauty, violet, watercress, wild ginger, wild strawberry, wood sorrel, yucca.

Anytime Edibles

dandelions, fern fiddleheads, miner's lettuce, sorrel, purslane, violets, primroses, roses, day lilies, wild onions, mullein, dead nettle, tansy, burdock, milkweed, lamb's quarters, chickweed, yarrow, watercress, mints, cattails, grape leaves, nasturtiums, squash family flowers, carnations, mums, calendula, geraniums, squaw cabbage, cacti, moss, lichens, bark (inner cambium layer), nuts, berries, honey, spring sap from trees (*EXCEPT LOCUST TREES WHICH ARE POISONOUS), acorns (boiled), pine tree nuts, guinea pig, hedgehog, possums, raccoons, lizards, snakes, ants, bees, grasshoppers, butterflies, caterpillars, worms, wasps cicadas, crickets, dragonflies, locusts, water fleas.

CAUTION: IDENTIFY AS EDIBLE ANY WILD FOOD BEFORE EATING IT

READY. AIM. FIRE!

If you're a first time or old-time gardener, you know that gardening is a crapshoot. By a crackling fire in your jamies with heavy sox on and with your stack of increasingly sophisticated catalogues, you dream of the garden you will create or recreate when the ground gets soft enough to dig up all those whatevers that didn't do anything and put in these here on page 62 that are the most beautiful, the newest, the most most. You order the young plants or seeds. You put them just where the books say they should be and--- sometimes they are terrific. Often they disappoint.

Most of us want a garden that thrives and delivers bloom that we can enjoy outside and in vases in our homes. The following is a list of almost (Nature is sovereign) sure-fire perennials that will at the least not disappoint you and at best delight you.

Let's start with "A."

Achillea otherwise known as Yarrow is a winner. It is an old-fashioned plant and looks its age. Nostalgically ferny and sometimes droopy (especially the red achillea), yarrow never seems to fail. I've planted it in the regular garden and in a spot where an old apple tree fell down. It thrived in both places, but it got huge when it was attempting to replace that old apple tree! Parts of it were 8 feet tall! Its stems were a big-toe around and the plates of dull gold in July and August were impressive. You can dry these broad, flat flower clusters for winter bouquets by just cutting some stems and letting them dry in your pantry.

I have a whole garden of Astilbes. I call it the Blake Garden after my son Blake who dug it for me. Astilbes can be grown in shade or in sun but they do like wet feet. I got my first Astilbe at our Garden Sale. Someone had donated a 4' by 4' clump that contained ONE red

Astilbe plant. (I told you I'm only giving you sure-fire hits.) A friend and I bought it and hacked it in two. You can do things like that to Astilbe. She's very resilient. I took my 2' square plant home and my other son Jesse dug me a big hole. I plunked her in and covered her with some dirt. She's bigger now than when we mutilated her. She was so reliable that the following year I got some white Astilbe and some pink Astilbe. Every year all of them sport many of their long-lasting pointy plumes for summer bouquets. After they bloom, their artfully divided foliage looks good, too.

Of course, I have to include day lilies (Hemerocallis) in sure-fire plants. They are never-fail. The deer come in every Spring and eat their tender shoots, but they rejuvenate and send up their sturdy stems with delicate lilies right on time.

You can have day lilies blooming from June to November if you read the catalogues and buy according to bloom time. The colors they offer now are exquisite. I have a regal purple one, a tangerine-colored one, a mossy pink one, a baby yellow one. They come in almost any color that can be hybridized from those old, original yellow and orange tiger lilies. Plop them in; forget them; they'll multiply. Now there's a good plant!

And plop in some Liatris in the middle of your sunny garden. This perennial multiplies and divides well. Originally I got two of them. In three years, through manual division (hack and replant in the Spring) I had almost 85 Liatrises! In some places they are called Kansas Gayfeathers. Kansas must have been gorgeous covered with all those tall spikes of lavender during the grueling Great Migrations of Pioneers in the late 1800's.

Hostas. What garden would be complete without these war horses? They are grown primarily for their white and biting green foliage. I haven't found a place where they wouldn't grow, but they are known as a Shade Plant. I got my first specimens when a builder let some of us into an estate that he was going to raze. The house had been built in the late 1800's by some New Yorkers as a summer home. The acreage had been completely rimmed by a 10' deep perennial border. The gardeners, for there must have been many, planted all the right plants. The rows of peonies, day lilies and hostas were all that remained, but we could imagine the multitudes of perennials and annuals which had been planted each Spring by the country gardeners for the city dwellers. We dug and lugged our treasures to our trunks for days. As I cradled the giant, blue leaves of the last Hosta sieboldiani in my arms, I looked at the house on the hill. The bulldozers had just rammed into the music room. Whose ears had heard that music? Whose eyes had glanced on the Hosta I held?

I love Lamium. If you have a shady or partly shady place which has defied Myrtle and Pachysandra, try Lamium. This ground cover is the best! It's got grey-green leaves riddled with silver. It's the only plant I know that is truly silver, like the metal. And it spreads. It's not evergreen, but who cares! It comes up early in the Spring and spreads rapidly, spreading all those lovely 1'-2' shimmering plants all over the area. Spikes of small, hooded yellow flowers are an extra bonus in the Spring. Other species of Lamium yield purple, red or white flowers, but the original yellow-flowered Lamium is the strong one.

Talk about Yellow. Coreopsis verticillata aka Tickseed is one of the only perennials which gives continual bloom all summer long. This Coreopsis is a big ferny bush-like plant that begins to bloom in late June and will bloom all the way through to September. What more could you want? Each of the hundreds of tiny stems has a petite little yellow daisy on it. The plant does get bigger and you can divide it, but it is never obtrusive. Last year we had a two-month drought. The only plant that didn't seem to suffer was Coreopsis verticillata.

I like plants that don't seem to suffer from the vicissitudes of Nature. Columbines are pretty good that way. The ones that I particularly like are the original, wild white Aquilegia. One got into my property about ten years ago and has self-sowed all over the place. In the Spring I'll find its graceful self dangling its white funnels in the stones in the pool area or in between the cracks of a brick walkway.

Golden Rod is hated by sneezers, but it's nice to have a golden clump of it around for late summer color.

Ornamental grasses come back like our lawns year after year. They are sure-fire, but watch out! Some of those swaying, willowy babies can get so tall and so wide that they can hide a 6 year-old! So plant accordingly.

Johnny Jump Ups jump up everywhere once you've planted one. I usually leave them in their hideouts.

Liriope is always there at the front of the garden or path no matter what you do. It does have great little lilac flowers for summer nosegays, but you have to really look through the curving, spiky leaves to find them.

Phlox will definitely come back, but you have to weigh her penchant for powdering herself against the panicles of bloom.

Oenothera (Evening Primrose) closes her butter yellow eyes every night, but she will be there and be there and be there during the day.

There are Peonies in Japan that are 400 years old, so you know that you should plant some of these beauties.

And my orange Oriental Poppies have been with me for over 15 years. That's sure-fire!

"He who has Sage in his garden will never die," states the old Persian proverb. I think that's because the whole decocted herb, in moderation, is so good for you. The little purple flowers are a slight boon. Sage spreads and gets craggier with age, but ages well in the garden.

Another herb, Santolina virens, is a reliable garden plant. I love to smell its pungent, green foliage.

It may take the Yucca plant a long time to bloom, but that Accent Plant stays with you. Mine took four years to bloom. When it did, the flower stalk was 6' high. My husband Steve "accidentally" mowed it down that year. The next year it came up, but didn't bloom. Steve "accidentally" mowed it down again. All summer long he made the Yucca part of his lawn. I'd like to say that it survived since we're talking about plants that will really perform no matter what. It didn't.

Barring Steve's lawnmower, the above sampling of perennial reliables are sure-fire. Order or buy some of them. You'll see.

But buy the crapshoot plants, too---the ones subject to the vicissitudes of Nature. You need the disappointments to be a real gardener.

A GARDENER'S DIARY

I started this Diary two years after I got into gardening. I had learned all the Latin names of the flowers in order to communicate internationally with gardeners. My gardening friends thought that was silly, but that's me.

When I re-read these scribbled notes, the overwhelming impression I have is---what a lot of WORK! Those of you who garden can identify.

1982

FEBRUARY 1982

2/16/82---Looked at the old stump down by the road and saw little stalks peeping out. Was glad to see the 28 days of below zero weather hadn't killed them all off!

2/18/82---Looked at whole garden; still some snow; ground frozen solid; but---primroses are up, little basal growth around delphiniums, dianthus, etc. Put wood ash around delphiniums, dianthus, lupines, sage, lavender, rue, santolina, etc. More bulbs are sticking out of the stump and the narcissus are starting to come up!

Noticed the wild flower (unknown to me) that I snatched from the pavement last fall at Caldor's is coming up. It had the most delicate foliage I'd ever seen---that's why I got out of the car and dug it out of the pavement. It was growing in the space between two pieces of concrete. I wiggled it and cajoled it out with its roots attached, hurried home and planted it in the deep loam of the stump.

I travel with a shovel in my car. If I see something, I screech to a stop, pull over, grab my shovel and dig it up. My trunk is always white with dried dirt. My dear mother says, "You're certifiable, Sandra. I'm going to have you probated!"

MARCH 1982

3/2/82----Was too cold to do anything in the garden. 10-20 degrees.

I am getting very antsy to get out and inhabit my gardens. Feb. 28 and March 1 were freezing---"in like a lion, out like a lamb!" Hopefully that'll be true this year.

Took a course at Pound Ridge Nursery in February on landscaping and perennials. Went over photos of the yard before there was any gardening. Now there are eight beds dug out of the yard by these small hands. The love of horticulture is so deep, I can't believe I've only been interested in it for 2 years. Always thought gardening was for old women who had nothing better to do.

3/12/82---It's ironic that this page in the diary has a bee skep on it as today Steve and I went to Ed Weiss and I got my observation hive. It's a beauty. Cost me $225.00 including the package of bees that will come in April. Ed put three used combs in the top and I like them MUCH better than the new virgin-white ones that came with the hive. His have a golden brown, seasoned look. I don't like new houses either. Give me one that has been seasoned with time and people (like my wonderful Victorian here). Ed's bees were out in the late afternoon sun. On one hive they hung in a beard about 2,000 bees strong. Ed approached the beard and held his hand out. The bees could have cared less. This helped Steve with his fear. I'm SURE bees know their keeper by his/her pheromone. They have such a keen sense of smell. Ed Weiss, however, doesn't agree with me.

3/23/82---The yellow, white and purple crocuses in the front yard are up and blooming! Like a miracle---one day nothing, next day full bloom. Hard as I try, I can't catch the bloom. Secret, they are, the blossoms. Very private.

Saw the first tiny lupine leaves.

The squirrels got MOST of the bulbs I put in around the old stump. Well, if the bulbs weren't to nourish the eyes, at least they nourished those quick, young, bushy bodies.

3/31/82---"In like a lion, out like a lamb." March began freezing; ended today with a gentle rain in the 50's. All the bulbs are up 4"-5"---the tulips, daffodils, hyacinths, narcissus. The little bulbs are all up, too. The thousands of scilla siberica are up but not blooming yet. I can see those little blue heads ready to poke out of the thin green spikes.

The santolina stems I cut and put in vermiculite two days ago have already rooted! No luck so far with the lavender stems.

Transplanted the rhubarb to a better spot. Yummy spring rhubarb boiled in a little water, lots of sugar and the sweet sop in a dessert bowl and in my tummy. Also transplanted centaurea and the rue. Boy, does that pretty bluish herb stink! No wonder we "rue" things. "If you don't come in for dinner right now, Sandra, you'll rue the day you were born."

I'm making a hedge of herbs along the garage--- perennial ones, of course.

APRIL 1982

4/6/82---Today April 6, 1982 Connecticut and the entire Northeast had a monstrous blizzard! The radio has already dubbed this the Blizzard of '82. LaGuardia, Kennedy and Newark airports are closed. Here in Ridgefield we have 12" of snow. The town is paralyzed. I woke up around 8:00 and couldn't see out of the bay window. That condition persisted until 5:00 this afternoon. Now at 9:00 P.M., it's snowing again---a straight down, no-nonsense falling. The temperature is 15 degrees tonight.

Many bulbs and perennials were up. I'm hoping they'll be protected by this "poor man's manure." I must say the <u>Farmer's Almanac</u> predicted snow for this time! They, also, predict frosts in May. The planets aligned in March. Maybe that's the cause of such unusual weather. My scilla siberica was just coming into bloom---a carpet of blue under the old copper beech tree. I hope they'll be okay.

Jesse and I are here alone and cozy. I'm making us Three Bear Porridge and the English Muffins with hamburger mustard that he loves. Blake went to Chris Rushton's and got stuck there. Steve flew out at 7:30 this morning for Columbia, S.C. and escaped the blizzard. Kathy is safe at Pitt. So there's no one to worry about. Jesse and I will get cozy and rejoice! Praise You, Jesus!

4/17/82---I hived the 10,000 honeybees in my new observation hive today and Steve installed them in the kitchen window. They made a beeline for the 10,000 scilla siberica that are in bloom!

4/18/82---My dear Kathy got home from college today and the first daffodil bloomed to welcome her! I do so miss her when she's away! When we took back her rented car, I saw some coltsfoot by the side of the road. Stopped, dug them up and have planted them by the driveway.

4/24/82---I have BLOOMING: daffodils, narcissus, hyacinths, scilla, crocus, anemone, dandelions, Johnny jump ups, ajuga, pulmonaria, forsythia. Everything except the platycodon and asclepias is up and will bloom.

4/25/82---Put in purple sage, silver santolina, lacey lavender in the herb garden by the side of the garage where I already have sage, rue, lavender, santolina. What great smells from these strewing herbs. Imagine how they cut the smells strewed as they were under the tables of those filthy medieval mead halls!

Put teucreum and santolina which I rooted from cuttings as a border in the upper garden.

Finished cleaning up all gardens and planted pansies in the side yard "rock" garden. Planted zepherantes, freesias, oxalis, ranunculus, monthretias, helium in various places.

Everything came through this TERRIBLE winter and seems the better for it! Like life if you persevere. Tulips are getting ready to bloom. The kale I planted last summer in the vegetable garden came through the winter and is flourishing. It's so gorgeous! Lots of parsley and onions came back. Did lose one heuchera (coral bells). As I look around the yard, I see lots of tree branches that have to be cleared away from Nature's own pruning all winter.

My bees are laying in a lot of nectar. I am keeping a daily journal of observations about them. I'm calling it <u>A Cosmos In My Kitchen</u>, as, indeed, it is a parallel universe.

MAY 1982

5/14/82---Since early May it has been sunny and warm (70 degrees) every day. Thus the gardens look beautiful!! I put in a Heath, Heather and Thyme garden in front of the Carriage House where we have our wonderful Bible Study every Sunday evening. Planted 6 heaths and 6 heathers (I'll get more in July when different varieties come in); 2 lemon thyme; 2 wooly thyme. Put a big statue of St. Fiacre, patron saint of gardeners, right in the middle of the new garden. Don't believe in church saints. Only believe in believer saints. He looks great there.

I, also, got a birdbath shaped like a shell for my bees. It's small and I put it on the ground near the entrance to the hive. It has many places around the rim for them to land and get their water to air condition the hive this summer. I painted "Pleasant Words Are Honey. Proverbs 16:14" on it. Also painted "God Gives The Increase" on a flat stone in the garden outside the kitchen. I cemented 2 cute tiles of partially eaten apples onto a plate and put it near my herbs. Then I fixed up a table, chair and some pottery and placed them in my shade garden so I could go there and relax and enjoy. I want to fix up the outside of the house (gardens, etc,) as pretty as I do the inside of the house.

Blooming in my garden now: convularia, dicentra, spectabilis and exima; daffodils and hyacinths (almost finished); tulips, grape hyacinths, anemone, euphorbia (incredible!), phlox divaricata, chives, sage almost in bloom, Johnny jump ups, scarlet salvia, sweet woodruff, pulmonaria, strawberries, lamium, jacobina, heathers, iberis, columbine, azaleas, rhodendrondons.

Have freshened-up the gardens with wood chips, hyponexed some things, weeded, tidied up, etc. The gardens are looking good and full. I have an incredible amount of work to do on the bank near the tennis court. Would like to put in a rock garden there.

My arms are swollen from three insect bites. Never had that before. There is a physical price to be paid for sticking your hands and arms into the dirt home of so many micro creatures.

Found two huge aquilegia buried under some evergreens near the pool and dug them out and planted them near the cabana. I have painted, papered and fixed up the cabana. It looks nice. Put up a Connecticut poster. The slogan on it is: "Better yet. Connecticut." How absolutely dumb!

5/26/82---When I came home from my prison ministry at Danbury Fed. Penitentiary, Steve was cutting the grass---IN THE DARK! He has physical scars on his body from cutting the grass! He will head the riding mower toward the old bushes up by the road, put his right arm across his eyes and head in! He always comes into the house with cuts and scratches from just mowing the lawn! Plus, he mows OVER rocks and roots. I'll hear zings and dinks and clanks and then I'll look out of the kitchen window a while later and he's got the mower turned upside down. He's banging away with a hammer at the blades. Obviously he's bent them in his zeal. The guy at the lawn mower repair place always says when Steve (frequently) brings the mower in for repair, "It's Mr. Silver who mows the Baja Trail up there on High Ridge." That's my man!!

The grass and all the gardens are lush and full after five days of rain preceded by four weeks of drought. The Johnny jump ups are all over in the grass from self-seeding.

My sage bush is a mass of buds. "He who has sage in his garden should never die," goes the old Persian proverb. All I really want is to bloom with wisdom. Those Oriental poppies are ready to bloom---fat, hairy buds with a crooked smile as befits its properties! Remember Ulysses' poppy-drugged men.

The roses that survived the winter have small buds. They'll probably bloom a month from now.

When I did the vegetable garden this year, I put in half vegetables and half flowers---cutting flowers like cosmos and dahlias, etc.

The tritoma and liatris that I transferred back into full sun are spreading and thriving.

The lovely phlox divaricata are still in bloom. I love them all and the reliable hostas!

"...for indeed it is impossible for any man to have any considerable Collection of noble Plants to prosper, unless he love them: for neither the goodness of the Soil, nor the advantage of the Situation, will do it, without the Master's affection: it is that which animates, and renders them strong and vigorous; without which they will languish and decay through neglect, and soon cease to do him service."
From A Complete Florilege by John Rea 1665

JUNE 1982

6/28/82---Have had an extremely busy month with my bees and bee journal and so have neglected this diary. My poppies came and went---not as nice as last year but still very many. Last year they bloomed with white columbine behind them, purple campanula medium to their right. The three stands together—brilliant orange, paper white and royal purple--- were glorious! But this year the columbine were finished when the poppies bloomed. The poppies came and went and now only the gorgeous, self-sowing campanula is blooming away.

I guess plants can do that---change their time.

The campanula was fuller and more numerous than last year. The lupine are still going---gorgeous purple! However, they are not as lush or as many or as tall-spiked as last year when the flower spikes were almost three feet tall. But it is a good bush and I am letting seeds ripen to give away to others who always marvel at this one.

The two types of coreopsis I have are blooming---better than last year. They have spread---yellow flowers, fat on long, sturdy stems. The lemon yellow oenothera flowers are spreading and showy. Delphiniums with their crinkly leaves (with some perennial blight on them) are crowded with full flowers. And the campanula persicifolia---blue and white---I keep taking off those cute bells that are dead and new ones come until Fall.

In the dead of last winter I put wood ash on the clematis vines and they were exquisite this year. Was worth the cold trip in the snow. I want to get more and more of these beauties!

The lysimachia is out. Here in Ct. they call it "circle flower"---well-named with myriads of flowers climbing around the stem starting at the ground and circling up to the top, entwining among the leaves.

My, the comfrey---symphytum---has such a delicate little flower for such an imposing plant! My lilies, the hemerocallis and lilium, are out---gorgeous orange, tangerine and others. Royalty for sure.

6/29/82---Steve dug up and de-clodded part of the yard for me. I wanted to put in a wild flower garden. Put in hundreds of tiny pink, yellow, blue and white flowers. I'll find out what they are later. All I know is--the wild flower bouquet takes no back seat to the cultivated flower bouquet. Plus the wild flowers last longer in water!

I dug up loads of black-eyed Susans from the tennis court bank where I got all the other wild flowers plus I went out into the country and got about 25 clumps of wild white daisies. So the wild flower garden should be great next year.

My sage has been blooming for a month---high and tiny purple flowers. May wisdom bloom in me as profusely! I pinch off some of these aromatic leaves occasionally, steep them in water and Mother and I have a cup of sage tea sweetened with raw honey. We sit at the kitchen table here and talk about everything. As with those you love, you are never at a loss for words. I'm so happy I can share this part of my life with her. She's been such an influence on me. I love her so!

Can't drink too much sage tea, though. Then it starts to poison you.

And I love the faithful centaurea.

Plus my black iris was....Well, there's no word grand enough to capture it. Carol F. took photos of them. She'll probably paint a huge O'Keefe-esque canvas from the pictures!

Oh, and around the blueberry bush the profusion of geranium lacastriense spreading everywhere is a tangled riot of pink.

JULY 1982

7/31/82---This month has been extremely busy. Lots of entertaining around the pool. I love having people over and cooking for them. We already had the big 125 people party for Jesse's Birthday. Have it every year. This year Rick F. and Bob S. got big watermelons, greased them, plopped them in the pool and the many children tried to get them up on the edge of the pool. They were so slippery that even the teenage boys had lots of trouble.

Steve and I got away for a week to Gloucester---how we love the North Shore!

But the gardens. Early in July the black-eyed Susans on the tennis court bank started blooming along with five or six other wild flowers. All July I have been stopping by the roadsides to dig up other wild flowers for the new garden. Most of the wild transplants seem to have taken. They are surprised that I water and fuss about them---they who bloom their little heads off anonymously beside highways and in distant fields. Some have died but I'm hoping they seeded and their progeny will show up next year. I'll continue putting wild flowers in that bed (25 ft. by 25 ft.) until it snows. I have to get a book on wild flowers so that I can identify them.

Today I pulled up about 20 Queen Anne's lace, some wild lythrum and some unknowns. It's such a hodge-podge back there by the vegetable garden, but that's nature.

I did put the Queen Anne's flowers in water that I colored green. I watched the white plates of lace turn green the next day. Osmosis. I'll have to do this for my grandchildren---if and when I have them.

Re: vegetable garden. A family of wood chucks (remnants of Sherman's-March-To-The-Sea) has decimated my vegetables!! They've stripped clean all the broccoli, the red cabbage, the green beans--so forget any of those. They have eaten to 4" high ALL zinnias, the giant and regular; have nibbled lots of asters, but never touched my lovely and profuse nasturtiums and everyone knows they are good to eat. A little peppery, however, which may explain a lot. So, vegetable-wise, what I may end up having are: tomatoes, parsley, onions, celery, squash and the corn may come through for me.

In bloom among the vegetables are: asters (deep and light pink, multi-flowered), nasturtiums, cosmos, red celosia, white dusty miller, blue salvia (the last three are a flag of color together), a few zinnias, lovely, stately gladiolas, Susans, mums (didn't pinch them back), coreopsis, phlox, 3 kinds of daisies that dominate all, boltonia latisquama, centaurea, tritoma. A nice show.

Made 3 of the most beautiful bouquets several days ago. 2 had gypsophilia and Queen Anne's lace and lavender allium---stunning. One that I did for the Bible

Study that we have every Sunday night in the Carriage House had liatris, phlox, pink bee balm, echinacea and gypsophilia. It was beautiful beyond words!

The first bloom of the roses was striking. Nothing since. I've heard said that roses, like women, are gorgeous when they first bloom in the spring; then are nice in the summer, but give a gorgeous goodbye bloom in the fall.

The hemerocallis have been lovely. I have double tiger lilies plus lilium which are white, pink, orange, yellow, etc. The astilbes in the Blake garden are thriving. Thank you, dear son, for digging that garden for me! The rudebeckia is 8 ft. tall this year! Also, the heaths and heathers are blooming in their own garden.

AUGUST 1982

8/21/82---My prizes this August are: the profuse, lavender-colored allium with the even more profuse red achillea hanging over and in and through it! Profuse is the word. Some heaths and heathers proffered their delicate blossoms and I love the feel on my bare feet of the wooly thyme (inching all over with its soft, tight tendrils). I got a caraway thyme. You can't believe it, but it smells exactly like caraway seeds. How do they do these hybridizations anyway?! And the smell of lemon thyme meandering in and out of the heaths and heathers. Really, a HEATH, HEATHER AND THYME GARDEN IS A MUST!

Of course, the hostas have been blooming all summer. What a reliable work horse. Various kinds: seiboldiei and the other more common ones.

The stately lilium are incredible! The Rothschild Lily is---incomparable! Tall stalks with white and red speckled, swept-way-back faces; white with rust-speckled and delicate pink bangs! I pick the bloom, bring it in and it lasts for 8 days. And, oh, the perfuming of the whole area! Praise the Lord for people who have scads of money and do good things with it.

The lavender keeps blooming and so does its exquisite cousin the blue salvia---straight stems of deep blue beside the red celosia combs and the white dusty miller. The first year I turned up my nose at annuals. Well, I'd have scant bloom without the huge, ever-blooming annual asters (deep and light purple and deep and light pink); without the red, orange, yellow, pink, white and salmon zinnias; without the ever-bearing, huge 5 ft. stalks of white nictotiana. And my cosmos! They are so tall they are reaching for the cosmos. Lovely, feathery foliage. Profuse blooms of white, pink, deep pink. I thought my beanstalks were tall. Any day now some local Jack will start climbing these old-fashioned cosmos stalks making such a show in the front of my vegetable garden!

8/23/82---The lowly marigold. How reliable, reliable.

There's a little lick of morning glories on the trellis that calls your attention to them. And those yellow marguerites!! They're like bushes. A must-have. The bee balm, asters, mums and the tall (mostly mildewed) phlox. The gloriosa daisies are still stunners. My roses (tea) are budding to give a fall show as are the polianthes tuberosa. And even though the glads fall over, there's little to match them as a cut flower. Some of my dahlia bushes are full and lush, but 4-5 of them died! I have gazanias and I like the little silver underbelly of them.

The pink mullein is still going as is the echinacea that is one of my favorites. I peel off the faded pink petals and use the cones for winter bouquets. I, also, have shown little Jesse how he can brush his fine blond hair with the sturdy combs. He's my constant companion in the garden. He plays with his trucks and guns and balls. We wander in and out of each other's mornings---I on my knees, Jesse running and chasing the wind. Thank you, Lord!

The baby's breath is 3 ft. by 3 ft. and still has some dainty stems. The 8 ft. high rudebeckias with their after-thought yellow flowers competed with the 8 ft. pool fence---and won.

Because this August has been extremely cold, my tomatoes are still green! Love those thinly sliced fried green tomatoes every night for dinner! Parsley, onions, celery are good. Some zucchini left. I really lost a lot this year. BUT I had a harvest, too. Praise Him.

SEPTEMBER 1982

9/14/82---My little bees. The woodcut on the opposite page of this diary is of "Beehives in a Garden." Irony again that this Metropolitan Museum Diary should be so filled with bee imagery just as my/our lives are being filled by actual bees. They give a gardener's advice for September:
"Be sure to tread the Leaves of Roots, as Red Beats, Parsnips, Carrots, and they will thrive after it...You must still bind your Collyflowers about with Straw as they begin to Head."
Mash down the leaves of root vegetables? I'll have to try that.

My bees sure love the sedum. Those feathery, pink blooms must have a lot of nectar. And the workers are pollen gathering on the giant hydrangea bushes that over the last century have grown into trees on our 3 acres. The pollen is white. They're paying attention to the cosmos now. Didn't in August when everything was plentiful. The bumblebees always pay attention to cosmos. They are there all day and finally fall asleep in them. Jesse and I pet them. Very docile. Nectar-drugged. My bees, also, like the CONES of the coneflower. They don't seem to go for the asters, zinnias, etc.

I've seen three colors of pollen: blue from the scilla under the old copper beech; white (from the hydrangea and red raspberry bushes) and yellow (both light and golden yellow) which is the most common color of pollen. My honeybees love the goldenrod. I know others sneeze and consider it a weed, but I think solidago is one of the best cut flowers. I make huge fall bouquets of white and pink hydrangea with huge spikes of goldenrod and loads of purple, pink and lavender asters stuck in.

The work horse coreopsis verticillata is still blooming. My wood-sculpture stump looks beautiful with the mums of yellow, red and white blooming all around it! The spoon mums in yellow are showy and lovely. There are so many worlds here!

9/17/82---Had some warm weather (85 degrees) about a week ago and it ripened some of my tomatoes! So now they are lined up on the long window sill here in the kitchen and I have them heaped in a deep, yellow and brown crock (which I make my cucumbers and onions in) right here beside the sink. So now we have fresh tomatoes every night for dinner. Because they hung on the vine green, green for so long due to the cold August, we had fried green tomatoes a lot. I love them.

This is the time of year (and into Nov.) when I particularly appreciate annuals. Everything else has sort of had its season. Some of the asters are as big as saucers. The cactus and decorative dahlias are sensational. Those tall, fall spikes of blue salvia, the staggered stalks of gladiolus, the talkative mouths of pointed and pink snapdragons.

When we lived in Edinburgh, I went out on Christmas Day and picked two snapdragons! Lots of these thrive in nippy weather. And it's coming. I have huge bouquets of hydrangea drying in water-less vases all over the house. Reminder of what's to come when "old man winter" (love that song by Steve) insists, "It's always going to be like this."

1983

MARCH 1983

3/26/83---I'm working on a book, <u>Incredible Edibles,</u> about all the unusual meats, flowers, insects, greens, etc. one can eat. That book takes me deeper into flowers, herbs, wild things.

I've already cleared away about half of the winter debris in the gardens and, Praise God, everything is coming back! The thousands of Siberian scilla were covered by dead, wet leaves. We just got them cleared away last week. The leaf-bound squill were yellow, but I'm sure they're all right.

My bees died about a month ago and I'm getting a new package in April. They love the dainty blue pollen of these squill. Blake and Steve raked and raked and raked our acreage as they do every spring. Then they carted away all of the wet, mashed leaves in that reliable blue tarp.

We've had a very mild winter so it will be interesting to see what effect that has on blooms. The coltsfoot I dug up last year has been up and blooming for weeks. Galanthus and crocus and winter aconite came up March 1! Deer got a lot (20-30) of my tulip bulbs. I've never had deer before. Blake said last fall he was raking and a big buck bounded across High Ridge and came into our yard! Oh, well, everything must have a little of everyone's.

March has been cold! I work outside on sunny days (only 5 so far) and my hands and face get numb! I pick against the pitted, frozen earth with red fingers.

The poppies love it all and look healthier the colder it gets!

You know how I love "invasives." The red achillea is all over. Sweet woodruff, bee balm, nepeta, campanula persicifolia. Would that they all took over like those do. Signs of everything except late platycodon.

A month ago I took in azalea and rhododendron branches to force into bloom. The white azalea is blooming. Same with the viburnum, jasmine.

Gardening, the husbanding of the earth, is one wonder and experiment after another. Perfect for an inquisitive, seeking mind. Perfect for peace, patience, cultivating fruits of the Spirit.

APRIL 1983

4/15/83---Today Lena and I planted 24 Ozark strawberry plants. On the tennis court bank I found an additional 24 wild strawberry plants that my bees brought in. I know every inch of that bank and they weren't there last year. Already I've seen 2, no 4, instances of gifts from my bees:

1. The strawberry plants on the bank.
2. The scilla siberica have multiplied by at least 1,000. The other years it was an increase of 200-300.
3. Johnny jump ups are "honeycombed" all throughout the lawn.
4. The boltonia latisquama is all over the place. I can hardly wait to get my new bees next Saturday.

4/17/83---The coltsfoot I put by the entrance to the driveway lived and has been blooming for about a month. The annual dusty miller in the old stump still looks alive from last year. Boltonia has spread all over the top of the stump---good---pretty pink flowers.

I'm anxious to see what my wildflower garden looks like this year. There are many strange looking shoots in there. I've looked through wildflower books and can't find pictures of what I dug up in the woods, fields and by the roadsides.

April 1, Steve and I were working near the stump and Lynn G. and her daughter came over and told us sheepishly that her daughter had taken many family portraits in front of our stump last Fall when all the mums were blooming around it. She showed us an album with the family pictures there in front of our stump. They all looked so good with the beautiful, fallen, broken, tangled, artistic tree stub in the background surrounded by bunches of mums. Someone who was being married at the Ridgefield Inn next door last summer asked me if they could have their wedding pictures taken around the stump. I said, of course. Makes me feel good to know that so many appreciate what was an eyesore. He had been a stately tree struck decades ago by lightning and only split wood and his stump remained when we moved in. Steve wanted to cart it away, but I insisted it was an artistic tangle of wooden beauty. I planted flowers and bulbs in it and around it. What was an eyesore is now eye-catching. Sort of what Jesus does to a life.

JULY 1983

7/24/83---Made some ravishing giant bouquets. In the one the base was baby's breath; then wild asters; orange day lilies; giant pink spears of liatris; pink and red bee balm; Queen Anne's lace; giant stalks of the bloom of the leeks (fast becoming my favorite flower and a definite favorite of my bees!); then double 9" across gloriosa daisies and yellow lilies. Wow, it was gorgeous!! The Bible Study people were praising the Lord because of the beauty. I have taken 2 huge bouquets to two parties recently for hostess gifts. Even though I hate to pick my beauties, I do love to give them away!

Amazing---on the other bank of the tennis court we have loads of hybrid red raspberries which are picture-perfect and taste delicious. They grow on sticky, picky red berry stems and the berries grow contained in pods that open. I never ate them and would never allow anyone else to eat them because they didn't resemble any berry bush that I had ever seen. I assumed they were poisonous. This year, though, they looked so tempting. I took a sticky stalk with berries in the pods all over the area to nurseries and no could identify it for sure. They all agreed they looked like red raspberries, but no one was bold enough to taste one and find out. Finally, a neighbor, Diane K., said, "Oh, yes, I have loads of them. They are red raspberries. Old man Lewis who owned all of this land 100 years ago sent his gardener to England to get them." Well, today I picked a colander full of the huge, luscious red berries and I made a crème anglaise to pour over them. Thank you England and Old Man Lewis.

7/29/83---Finally---I got a little bloom from the blue hydrangea that I cut back 3 years ago. I didn't realize that next year's flowers come from this year's canes. That bush really chastised me for that mistake.

I have much blooming now. I love the huge plates of the gold achillea. Am bringing lots of them in and drying them for winter bouquets. I'll do that with the blue and white/pink hydrangea.

Some wild flowers are blooming. But most of the wild flowers didn't come back.

My hoped-for wild flower garden was a failure.

1984

APRIL 1984

4/17/84---When I read in this diary what was blooming last year at this time, I'm amazed! Don't have nearly as many blooming in mid-April this year! Unlike the winter of '82-'83, this winter of '83-'84 has been long, cold, unrelenting. It shows on the plants. I've seen one Johnny jump up. The daffodils are weeks away from trumpeting. Scilla siberica barely starting. Coltsfoot a week old. Crocus have bloomed as have the pushkinia. Galanthus, aconite, ajuga still very embryonic. But it'll all come. That's the promise!

I've only been able to work out in the yard three (!) days the entire spring! I usually have been out in the garden for a least a month by now.

Have cleaned up 6 of the gardens. Have 6 to go. Much is spreading—love those invasives! Am dividing and transplanting shastas, campanula, achillea, evening primrose, etc.

Have had loads and loads of thorns, big and small, in my hands. Each night I have to take a needle, sterilize it with a match, and dig them out. My nails are down to the quicks. Surely these are the hands of a manual laborer!

4/19/84---The Heath, Heather and Thyme Garden with the big Scotch Broom behind it looks fabulous! That old greenhouse that used to be there in front of the Carriage House left a lot of foundation stones to be covered. I've begun covering them with different types of sedum. I don't want to get too many themes going there. I like the Scottish theme of Heath, Heather and Thyme (after all, we lived in Edinburgh for a year!), but I have to cover those foundation stones with something. During the winter the heaths and heathers were beautiful---red and orange and silvery against the snow. They are a great and colorful evergreen. Why don't more people use them?! Since mid-March I have a Springwood white and a pink heather blooming.

Gunilla Segerblad is here with us from Sweden. She hasn't worked with me in the garden yet like my wonderful Lena Arvidsson did. She's less hearty and more delicate.

Praise You, Lord, for Your creation. Blake, Jesse and I watched Zeferelli's <u>Jesus Of Nazareth</u> tonight. Truly the finest movie ever made about the life of Jesus. Thank you, Zeferelli. We all wept, prayed and felt Your Holy Spirit.

6/27/84---Two years have passed since I made the 6/28/82 entry. My gardens have multiplied. I've dug 2 more big gardens and 1 small one. The gardens started April 1, 1980. I awakened and said, "I want every plant here in my yard that grows from Maine to Florida." (April fool?) Just like that. It was a sudden thing. No prior preparation. But that's how I get into all the many things I get into---suddenly.

The gardens now require little weeding. They are very full and only require good edging. The upper garden was gorgeous in the Spring---100's of sweet woodruff flowers and white, white/purple and purple violets and hundreds of ornithagolum poking up with splayed leaves with bloodroot running all through everything. The textures in that garden are nice---lots of ferns, hostas, tiger lilies, sweet woodruff, chrysanthemums, symphytum---ferny, pokey, spiky, full, big leaves. A nice blend.

Last year dear Lena dug a garden for me near this shade garden. I call it the Lena Garden. I was chairman of the Plant Sale and bought loads of left-over plants to plant in it. In January I had planted some pink campanula medium seeds (Canterbury bells). Last summer I put out small plants of them. They grew, survived the deer that ate them in the spring and then grew back. Now for several weeks I've had unbelievable stalks laden with 4" bells. No, they're bigger than that! I have in the Lena Garden large stands of the Pearl, bee balms, phlox and lythrum, but there's still room for more.

The garden next to the vegetable garden is gorgeous. The gigantic red bee balm now blooming there is so thick you can't see the ground. That garden is chocked full of tritoma, coreopsis, lysimachia, cimicifuga, filiipendula (Prairie Queen), etc. Fertilized the purple lupine once and it's done great. The poppies were, as usual, outstanding. This year for the first time the pink one I put in bloomed.

In our garden club's big Flower Show I won: Two Firsts for a lysimachia and a campanula glomerata. Two Seconds for my black iris and a pink campanula. Two Honorable Mentions for a miniature rose tree and 5 perennials.

My new love this year is saponaria---masses of bright pink blossoms. My bees love my blooming thyme. I love them, my Family, the Lord and Bloom Time.

1985

MARCH 1985

3/14/85---This second and third week of March I have been out in 40 degree, bright sun weather clearing away winter debris from the gardens. You do have to keep the dead cleared away from the tender living. It's so much easier later on. I came in the house with hands so cold I could barely move them, but I got away all the weeds! Like those weeds sin spreads throughout with tenacious roots at first and then it gets established. They (it) can, however, with great persistence and patience be controlled. Better to get it at the beginning though.

Of course, the thrill of discovery at Tooie's new place has been tremendous as we watched the woods fill with daffodil shoots, bloom with galanthus and shimmer with the deep blue myrtle flowers. You, O Lord, have given to her so abundantly!

"In Marche and in Aprill, from morning to night:
In sowing and setting, good huswives delight.
To have in their garden or some other plot:
To trim up their house, and to furnish their pot."
From <u>Five Hundreth Pointes Of Good Husbandry,</u> Thomas Tusser, 1573

Gardens have ALWAYS been for Beauty and for Sustenance.

1986

MARCH 1986

3/20/86---Went out the day after St. Patrick's Day (3/18) and most of the things in one perennial bed that gets full sun were up! Myosotis (100's), red achillea (100's), campanula persicifolia (had scores of tiny babies), Papaver, sticks of valerian, shasta daisies, campanula glomerata, buds of tight sedum spectabile. Even saw several tiny Johnny Jump Up leaves! Plus uncovered, still under some dirty leaves, pads of violets.

Spent an hour picking those heart-shaped leaves. Then brought them in and we had a delicate wild greens salad for dinner. Yum!

Saw some tulips. Thinned some ornamental allium to give Tooie a nice start-up clump. Weeded the wild ajuga. Pretended I was an ajuga being torn out tangle by tangle. I lay on the earth with my face against it.

Then on my back with my face to the 65 degree sun. The long and short of it---I woke up the next day with a chest cold that I'm determined NOT to get.

1987

MARCH 1987

3/87---I see the last entry was March of last year. I'm kind of winding down with this garden diary, I think. Also, saw that I was getting a cold last March. Well this month I got pneumonia for the first time. I was out weeding in the Lena Garden and I could feel the cold creeping into my bones. Palpably feel it, but I stayed there for hours anyway.

Next day I had a fever. Fever persisted and was finally diagnosed as pneumonia. Who says colds and pneumonia don't come from being cold!

And who says there's not small prices to be paid for the fruit and beauty of the earth!

MID-WINTER HERB BROTH

For most of A.D. history, "herbe" meant "grass" or all the green stuff that covers the earth. But mankind has always known the medicinal and culinary value of those types of earth coverings that we now know as herbs.

The medieval monks were the keepers of gardens of herbs and thus were consulted for all kinds of ills and diseases.

"A little parsley for that bad breath of yours." (We still garnish with that herb in homage to the monks' advice.)

"A little hyssop for your pain." (Jesus was offered hyssop on the cross.)

"A little mandrake for your sexual dysfunction." (They probably didn't put it that way.)

Nevertheless, herbs, and plants and trees have played an important part in the history of medicine. So we know that herbs are good for us. They have mysterious substances and qualities that heal and promote good health.

In the wintertime most of us will agree that our bodies become sluggish. For the winter blahs and just for fun, I often go out to my herb garden in, oh, January. There in the cold earth or under the soft snow some of my herbs are still okay. Often I can find some limp parsley, some chives, maybe a little lemon balm not winter-killed. Always I can gather the teeny thyme leaves, the pungent sage leaves (I'll boil them separately and have the infusion as a tea with honey) and I can always dig up a few garlic cloves and find some Egyptian onion bulbs.

Take whatever herbs you can scrounge into the house. Chop them up all together. (You can use supermarket herbs, but it's not as challenging.) Boil a strong chicken or beef broth for 10 minutes. Put the herbs into the broth. Boil for several minutes. Pour the tonic into a good coffee mug. Sit in a cozy chair with your feet up. Open Augustine's <u>Confessions</u> and smile.

LINGUINI AND ASPARAGUS

I was thinking that you would probably become so engrossed in Augustine's classic book that dinnertime will be upon you before you know it. So here's a quick and tasty pasta that will allow you lots of time with the Bishop of Hippo's confessions.

I love asparagus. But I keep serving it to one of my very best friends Beryl. Every time those straight green spears appear on her plate, she looks at me and says, "You know I don't eat asparagus, Sandy." I think I keep serving it to Beryl because I can't imagine that there is even one person who doesn't like this tender stalk.

Before asparagus was used as a food, people used it as a curative for toothaches, bee stings, dropsy and heart trouble. The ancient Greeks didn't cultivate asparagus as far as we know. They probably just picked and boiled the wild asparagus that grew around them. But the ancient Romans have left instructions for cultivating asparagus that are very similar to how we do it today. The Romans, also, dried asparagus in the sun, then stored it for out-of-season use. To eat the dried spears, they quickly boiled them in water. I'll have to try that and see how it tastes.

If you ever get a hankering to plant a bed of asparagus, make sure you're going to be in the neighborhood for a long time. They remain productive for 30-40 years! You have to have male (stamen) plants and female (pistil) plants because the individual spear does not contain both pistils and stamens as do most plants.

To explain what I mean: look at a big lily flower or you can look at the common tiger lily that grows by the side of the road. You'll see those tall stamens sticking up with the pollen on top of them. That's the male part of the plant that bears the pollen which is the seed of the plant. Buried way down in the center of the lily is the female part of the plant, the pistil. Most plants contain both male and female parts. The honeybees and other insects have to brush by the stamen with the pollen on top to get down into the heart of the plant where the nectar (and the pistil) is. While gathering their nectar, the bees will get that pollen on their furry little bodies. They will then drop some of that male pollen into the female pistil and "pollinate" or fertilize the plant. Sounds familiar, doesn't it?

With the asparagus, the male and female spears have to be growing near each other so that the wind, birds and insects can take the pollen from the male stalks and carry it to the pistil of the female stalks. Get it? It's really all about the birds and the bees (and that is the origin of that saying).

The bunch of asparagus spears in this recipe, male or female who can really tell, gives this sauce the ability to stand up to that big burly linguini.

Serves: 4-6.

2 Tbsps. olive oil
2 Tbsps. butter
2 garlic cloves, minced
1 bunch fresh asparagus spears, cut into 2" pieces
1 large onion, separated into rings
10-14 fresh mushrooms, sliced
Salt and pepper well
1 can Original Recipe Del Monte Stewed Tomatoes
Couple good dashes of Tabasco* Sauce
Couple good dashes Worcestershire Sauce
1 pkg. linguini

Melt the olive oil and the butter together in a pan over medium heat.
Add minced garlic. Saute until the garlic flavors the oil (about 1 minute).

Add the fresh asparagus, onion rings and sliced mushrooms. Mix them up.
Salt and pepper to taste. Saute for about 7 minutes.
Add the can of Stewed Tomatoes and the dashes of Tabasco and Worcestershire Sauce. Saute for about 15 minutes. Remove from heat.
As the sauce is simmering, boil the linguini. Drain.

To Serve: Spoon the sauce over the linguini. I always like grated Asiago or Parmesan on it. A chewy bread is always great with this pasta.

*Edmund McIllhenny began planting some hot pepper seeds that he had obtained from Central America right after he and his family returned to Avery Island, Louisiana at the close of the Civil War. When the plants matured, McIllhenny began experimenting with pepper sauces. In 1868 he found a concoction he liked. So did everyone else. Tabasco Sauce in those cute little "perfume" bottles took New York City palates by storm in the 1870's. Amazingly, direct descendants of Edmund McIllhenny still own and operate Tabasco brands and the worldwide company is still based on Avery Island.

REALLY GOOD GARLIC BREAD

This is an easy accompaniment to your pasta dinner. I really like this Garlic Bread.

4 garlic cloves, crushed
3 Tbsps. butter
3 Tbsps. olive oil
1 loaf good crusty bread, halved
A handful of fresh parsley, chopped

Place the crushed garlic in your smallest pan. Add the butter and olive oil.
Blend the butter and oil over low heat. Your kitchen will be filled with that good garlic aroma.
Under the broiler, lightly toast the bread halves. Remove from heat.
Brush each half of the toasted bread with the garlic butter. Re-heat under the broiler for a couple of minutes. Sprinkle with the parsley.

To Serve: Cut the slices and listen to the raves.

Note: Garlic is a member of the Onion (Allium) family. There is not a cuisine on the earth that doesn't use one of the 325 members of this smelly family. Their bulbs which are just modified stems are amazing! Each garlic, onion, or shallot bulb carries within it next year's flower, stem, leaves and roots in embryonic form.

This food family has been beloved for thousands of years. During the building of the pyramids of Giza in c. 2500 B.C., the workers' daily diet was loaded with garlic and onions. Even then they knew that the onion prevents stomach disorders and dysentery.

Hats off to the whole Allium family---to the red onions, the yellow onions, the white onions, the shallots, the scallions, the sweet onions, the pearl onions, the Egyptian onions, the leeks and the wild onions. And a special bow to you, Sir Garlic.

MEMENTO FLORI

I remember. Every spring I remember those who have given me so many of the perennials in my gardens. I remember Pat's chock-full-set-in-squares garden. She and her husband worked the garden and took in boarders. She gave away plants like street vendors push flyers. "I thought I gave away all of this Leopard's bane (Doronicum) for the Plant Sale last year, but look at these!" She made me take them-- the spring-flowering, yellow daisies with green heart-shaped leaves that are now competing for room among the insistent evening primroses (Oenothera). As we left her garden, she plucked up 8-10 shallow-rooted Forget-me-nots (Myosotis) dotted with bluish-pink flowers. Years later they are still all over my yard every spring. I dig them up and plant them in a garden patch. Next year they forget where they were last year.

Remembering the yellow Doronicum brings to mind the modest yellow flowers of the tall Jerusalem artichoke (Helianthus tuberosus). It's not an artichoke nor is it from the Holy Land, but this weedy-looking plant yields some of the best-tasting tubers in America. Plus it is the only plant source of insulin. Donna gave me about ten plants from her small, prim garden over ten years ago. She had deep brown hair flat down to her waist and a certain delicate nature. I was surprised she gardened. We stood on her deck as she put on gloves to dig up the Jerusalem artichokes. Every time I dig for the knobby tubers I remember that she committed suicide from that same deck. I pray for her soul as my ungloved fingers probe the deep brown earth. For to remember garden gifts is to remember people and lives.

I remember the day Beryl gave me all the garden heliotrope (Valerian) that had wandered from her small, English-perfect garden into her driveway. This ferny-leafed plant offers clusters of white-pink flowers in early summer that are excellent for bouquets. It spreads all over by underground runners, but I could care less. Everywhere it is is perfumed. Its longevity and sweetness are reminders of the long and sweet friendship between me and Beryl.

I remember the day Hawsie drove up in her station wagon with a 4'x6' glob of earth filled with gooseneck strife (Lysimachia chlethroides). "You said you wanted invasives, Sandy. These invade!" With difficulty we plopped the little garden on top of my wheelbarrow. When she left, I pushed it to the back of my property and eased it off. There it sat and there it has flourished and invaded. But I love the fact that from mid to late summer each stem yields a long-lasting white flower cluster curved like a goose's neck. Hawsie has since spread her wings for Europe.

I remember when we lived in Edinburgh, we had a few flowers in our backyard. At Christmastime the weather was so mild that I picked two snapdragons. We had several money plants (Lunaria) beside the garden shed. My grandmother Meme loved money plants and would harvest the seeds. I took an envelope-full of seeds when we left Europe. Every year I wonder at the miracle of nondescript blue flowers slowly turning into green and then stunning silver dollars. It's worth paying real money for this plant just to observe that transformation!

I remember laughing Lena from Sweden who dug and planted with me for a whole year. I remember the builder who gifted so many of us with plants from an estate to be bulldozed. I dug and dug for days and my car was black with dirt as I brought home Japanese peonies and Hosta sieboldiana. I remember Mildred's 50-year old garden and her 81-year old hands as she handed me some Boltonia latisquama that has lived ageless in my aging garden.

Each year I see so many of my old flower friends. Each plant and flower fragrance reminds me of some person, some place.

Good gardens consist of bought plants and "got" plants. I remember. I remember the flower gifts and the givers. Give.

REUNIONS

I just came back to Connecticut from Pittsburgh. I was there for a high school reunion. Several years before the reunion, I went back to Zaleski, Ohio, where my grandmother had had a summer home. I had not been there in twenty-five years. Meme had a prize garden. Summers, as a child, I would go into the garden early in the morning when the southern Ohio heavy dew was still on the grass. My feet and legs wet with the world of the night, I'd bury my small face in Meme's huge pink hollyhocks or play "loves me, loves me not" with her white shasta daisies. Meme always got up before me. She would have already thrown the contents of the chamber pot on the roses. Bending over her flowers in her flowered dress, she'd call my attention to a worm or a seedling or give me a bite of curly lettuce with the dirt still on it. As I ate the gritty green, she'd say matter-of-factly, "Have to eat a ton of dirt in your life, Sandy."

When I went back to Zaleski, I walked where her garden was. It had reverted to weeds and wild wheat. As I marked the area, a few pickers and burrs scratched my bare legs. I searched the ground between the weeds for some remnant of all that beauty and cultivation, some small survivor.

Unlike Matthew Arnold in his poem on mutability ("Thyrsis"), I found nothing. During Arnold's backward journey, he had found "The tree! The tree!" which made him believe there were some things which were immutable. But Meme's garden and Meme are gone. They live only in my memory and when I am gone, they will live no more.

In Pittsburgh some of my high school classmates had died. There was a special "In Memoriam" section in our Reunion Book dedicated to them. Some had died of cancer, others by accidents, suicides, diseases. As I read their names, I saw their faces fresh with high school still on them.

But most of us had returned, had survived, had even flourished. Like hardy perennials we had sprung back again to mingle, to laugh and to remember. And we all loved coming back, being back.

It was not a sad thing. Going to Meme's gone garden was not sad. The Reunion and Meme's gone garden are simply monuments to memory and memory is simply the fragrance of flowers past.

A FEW THOUGHTS ABOUT A FEW FILMS

THE LILIES OF THE FIELD

1963
STARRING SIDNEY POITIER AND LILIA SKALA
PRODUCER AND DIRECTOR RALPH NELSON
BASED ON THE NOVEL BY WILLIAM E. BARRETT
SIDNEY POITIER WON THE ACADEMY AWARD FOR
BEST ACTOR FOR THIS FILM

Worry, anxiety, depression and accidie. Accidie is the boredom that leads to emptiness and ennui. It was one of the Seven Deadly Sins in the Middle Ages. According to the Bible, the contemplation of lilies can actually be an antidote for such manifestations of spiritual hunger. In Matthew 6: 25-34 the 1st century Jesus talks about 21st century angst:

"Therefore I tell you, do not worry about your life, what you will eat or drink, or about your body, what you will wear....See how the lilies of the field grow. They do not labor or spin. Yet I tell you that not even Solomon in all his splendor was dressed like one of these....So do not worry...your heavenly Father knows you need these things. But seek first the kingdom and His righteousness and all these things will be given to you as well. Therefore, do not worry about tomorrow."

He's saying in the Sermon on the Mount, "Don't worry about your life and what's going to happen and where you're going to live and what you're going to eat and to wear. Look at the lilies of the field. They don't agonize, but they are better dressed than King Solomon was."

You've seen those day lilies by the wayside. They break the earth, bud and bloom their glorious heads off in the wake of gas fumes, globs of tar, bad soil and winter salt. How do they survive? How did they get there? They're so beautiful but they aren't cultivated, worried about and agonized over. They're just happy, carefree drifters like Sidney Poitier was in the film. The nuns were spiritual settlers. Together they learned the "Lessons of the Lilies": Don't worry. Don't take care. God will take care.

Let's all sing together now. One, two, three.

"Amen. Amen.

Amen. Amen. Amen."

DAYS OF WINE AND ROSES

1962
STARRING JACK LEMMON AND LEE REMICK
PRODUCER MARTIN MANULIS
DIRECTOR BLAKE EDWARDS

Two of our society's prized gifts for anniversaries, birthdays or just plain serendipity days are a bottle of wine and a dozen roses---preferably long-stemmed. Wine has always meant celebration. The fruit of the vine has been around almost as long as we have. The early alcoholic drinks were made of grain mashes and fruit ferments.

By far the most famous intoxicating beverage for the common folks of long ago was made from honey. It was called "mead" and the mead halls of <u>Beowulf</u> and other early writings ring with the sound of drunken reveling and fighting.

The Romans had a saying, "Veritas Vino" ---"There is truth in wine." By this they meant that when a person is drunk, they tell the real, real truth. Now, I don't believe that for a minute. Being intoxicated or drugged does take away inhibitions. If you don't like someone, you might tell her that if you are drunk more readily than when you are sober. But the drunk or drug addict is not the person they really are. They are the people the drink or drug makes or has made them be. I don't drink and I never have. Should I become drunk, it would be a dramatic departure from what I really am. If I were drunk daily, I would be daily a different person than I really am. So Veritas Vino only applies to letting go of some inhibitions. Drugs and drink let the wild dogs out, so to speak. Morality is all about attempts to keep the wild dogs in their kennels, about inhibiting our fallen nature. If the veneer of

126

morality and civilization is scratched away, it's pretty ugly underneath.

In the mead halls many a knight fortified with many swigs of megethlin (mead) fought and died and was buried in the olde sod as his ladylove laid a rose upon his hasty grave.

For roses have always meant remembrance and love. They are the prime flower. The rose symbolizes eternal beauty, love and womanhood. Elegant, exquisite yet armed with thorns, she is coveted and daunting.

In the film, Days of Wine and Roses, Lee Remick and Jack Lemmon give riveting performances of a married couple who took the rose of love and ill-combined it with the gift of mead. The result was a mash of woundings and revelings that agonizingly demonstrates the need for restraint and awe when handling the age-old elixir and the age-less flower.

CACTUS FLOWER

1969
STARRING WALTER MATTHAU, INGRID BERGMAN
AND GOLDIE HAWN
PRODUCER M.F. FRANKOVICH
DIRECTOR GENE SAKS
GOLDIE HAWN GOT AN OSCAR FOR BEST
SUPPORTING ACTRESS FOR THIS FILM

They are really amazing plants, the cacti (plural for cactus). They are indigenous to the Southwest United States and are not found in the deserts of any other continent. Every cactus in a desert setting that is depicted on any canvas or child's drawing is always an American cactus in our American desert.

The cactus that children and artists draw is usually the sugharo cactus that has been tapped by many a cowboy and Indian for its huge supply of water. If you are ever in our desert and in need of water, just hack away at one of sugharo's huge arms or its trunk. You can survive forever on the hoarded water.

But the astonishing thing about cacti in general is that such ugly, prickly, rather ungainly plants actually produce flowers. And some of the most magnificent flowers on the planet are cactus flowers. Everyone is familiar with the Christmas cactus and its cascades of bloom, but there are vibrant, orange, feathery flowers and delicate pink quadruple flowers produced by cacti. There is one cactus in Central America that produces its flowers once every 100 years! Generations of botanists wait for this event.

Those who have cacti know how hard it is to get them to bloom. The technical phrase is " Cacti are SHY."

The combination of the prickly exterior and the possible bloom is what inspired the title <u>Cactus Flower</u>

128

in this movie with Walter Matthau (naturally the cactus) and Ingrid Bergman (who made him bloom at last).

Maybe there's a cactus in your life. Maybe he or she is very prickly on the outside but you know he is really a pussycat on the inside. Maybe he keeps people away with his barbs and thorns? Maybe she's a loner way out there in the desert. Don't give up on him or her.

Give him the right temperature, just the right amount of moisture, lots of TLC and he'll eventually bloom. You don't want any one you love to be "destined to bloom and die and lose their fragrance on the desert air," do you. Of course, you don't. So keep trying. He'll bloom.

Unless you've got a real SHY one. Then you have to work even harder!

THE SECRET GARDEN

1949
STARRING MARGARET O'BRIEN AND DEAN
STOCKWELL
DIRECTOR FRED M. WILCOX
SCREENPLAY BY FRANCES HODGSON BURNETT AND
ROBERT ARDREY
FROM THE BOOK IN 1911 BY FRANCES HODGSON
BURNETT

A secret garden is usually a garden hidden away some place on your property that gives you delight and respite. Mine is behind the garage in a small place shaded by a huge evergreen and surrounded by old and tangled rhododendrons. The ground is always covered with a bed of soft pine needles, good loam for my wild jack-in-the-pulpits. I sneak a peek at him upright in his striped pulpit. The Indians ate them. I have lots of bi-colored Solomon's seal (dig up the root and it looks like the seal of a king) shooting up from a bed of soft, ferny sweet woodruff (it gives May Wine its special flavor). On the right there near the googols of silvery Lamium are four or five Umbrella Plants with their waxy May apples. As a child, I'd pretend the serrated leaves were real umbrellas. A small bed of bloodroot (witches are always associated with this sanguinarian) next to some wild, pink-flowered geraniums and little bits of this and that delight me especially in the Spring.

Secret gardens in the movies are places where the run-down becomes rehabilitated. I much prefer the 1949 screen version of The Secret Garden to the 1987 one with Derek Jacobi (who was incomparable as Claudius in I, Claudius).

The 1949 adaptation of the Frances Hodgson Burnett classic starred Margaret O'Brien, Elsa Lancaster, Dean Stockwell and lots of other greats. I read this book to my children. Adults and children thrill to this story as Margaret O'Brien single-handedly brings the garden back to life and at the same time everyone in that whole oppressive estate is transformed.

If you can get a copy of this film, watch it. You will appreciate the young O'Brien's beguiling sweetness. It may inspire you to create a secret garden of your own. There has to be some spot of earth or bit of porch that you could transform into a patch of wonder and secrecy.

DRIVING MISS DAISY

1989
STARRING MORGAN FREEMAN AND JESSICA TANDY
DIRECTOR BERESFORD
WON THE ACADEMY AWARD FOR BEST PICTURE IN
1989

If any movie star ever looked like a daisy, it was Jessica Tandy. She had the delicacy and strength and flat-out unfaded beauty of a white daisy. And white she was in contrast to her black chauffeur, Morgan Freeman, who drove her here and there decade after decade. The two opposite skin colors gradually became one in spirit. Color differences ceded to soul recognition which is how it's all supposed to work.

The daisy is, hands down, the most egalitarian of all flowers. She grows proudly in the back of your garden as the sturdy-stemmed Shasta. She cowers lowly on your border as the miniature Aster. She stands boldly in your tub as Marguerite. She dangles lazily among the Doronicum as Anthemis. In fact, the daisy belongs to the plant group that contains the most plants, Compositae. A daisy can be white, yellow, pink, red, bluish or purple. She is the longest-lived of bouquet flowers.

Go out on a nice, high-sun summer day. Pick a huge bouquet of flowers. Get some orange day lilies, some pink hydrangeas, some blue liropes, some red achillea, some white phlox, some yellow lysimachia and some white daisies. Arrange them in a large vase or pitcher. Enjoy them on your table for several days. Keep wiping up the pollen and petals that fall onto the table. Sooner rather than later, it's time. The water begins to smell, the flowers are gone. It's time to throw them out. But wait!

Not everything is dead and dying. Look and you'll see those members of the daisy family are still good to go. Their stems may be the worse for wear. Wash them off. Make a little bouquet of them. They'll still delight and look great even though they are old.

Just like Jessica Tandy in the movie.

STEEL MAGNOLIAS

1989
STARRING JULIA ROBERTS, SALLY FIELD, DOLLY PARTON, SHIRLEY MACLAINE AND OLYMPIA DUKAKIS
DIRECTOR HERBERT ROSS

Magnolias! The very word evokes the South and languid days and humid nights filled with the scent of these magnificent flowers. The Southern writers Tennessee Williams and Harper Lee wove magnolias into their writings as did Eudora Welty and William Faulkner.

The magnolia tree can grow up to 60 feet tall. In my town of Ridgefield we have several huge ones that stop my car every late Spring with their thousands of white/pink tulip-shaped blooms. I once stopped right under one of these beauties. Blake, Jesse and I sat there for about 5 minutes surrounded, enveloped in an assertive beauty that one associates with delicacy. How strong beauty is, I thought. Strong like Truth. Strong like the Love I felt for my young boys as the three of us looked up into the silent canopy.

The original trees came from China. By the 1600's they were prized in Britain. Magnolias get their name from Pierre Magnol (1638-1715), the French botanist, who studied and cultivated them.

Rosalind Carter was, I think, the first "Steel Magnolia" whom I remember. She was so named because she was a woman with a soft Southern accent who fiercely defended her beleaguered husband. The term obviously means a Southern woman who looks on the outside delicate like the magnolia flower but is really hard as nails on the inside.

That's not a compliment in some circles, but it befits the characters in the movie <u>Steel Magnolias.</u>

Julia Roberts didn't persevere until the end, but Dolly Parton, Shirley MacLaine, and crew showed the grit and humor accent-challenged women need to survive.

I really think "magnolia" is the wrong flower to describe those types of Southern women. Maybe "Steel Portulaca," "Steel Crape-Myrtle" or....

SPLENDOR IN THE GRASS

1961
STARRING NATALIE WOOD AND WARREN BEATTY
PRODUCED AND DIRECTED BY ELIA KAZAN
WON THE ACADEMY AWARD FOR BEST ORIGINAL
STORY AND SCREENPLAY

William Inge the playwright won an Oscar for this 1961 film that debuted the scattered Sandy Dennis. Warren Beatty was a young heartthrob who had splendored in the grass a lot and had the stains on his jeans to prove it. It was directed by the great Elia Kazan (<u>America! America!</u>). Natalie Wood gave her usual wooden performance but she did splendor in the grass enough to heal her heart in this teen film.

But what is there to say about grass? It's not a flower (<u>Cactus Flower</u>); it's not a tree (<u>Steel Magnolias</u>); it's not a beverage (<u>Days of Wine and Roses</u>); it's not a member of the Compositae family (<u>Driving Miss Daisy</u>); it's not a Biblical lesson (<u>Lilies of the Valley</u>); and it certainly doesn't grow clandestinely (<u>The Secret Garden</u>).

What you can say about grass is that it is that amazing and splendid plant that grows all over this planet in every climate and continent. If you go back to where you lived decades ago, the house will be changed, the trees will be gone, the gardens will be paved over, but the yard, the lawn, the GRASS will still be there!

Grass endures and it even comes back once it's gone.

If your young boys played baseball so much in one part of your yard that they wore away the grass at home plate, at the pitching mound and at first base and if your husband grouched about those bare places and you worried about those pocks on your lawn, you needn't have. When the children's rooms are always neat and there are only two people at the dinner table and the house is always clean and it's really quiet and you look out the window---there's the grass.

There's grass where those bare spots used to be.

If it had a mind to, grass could take over the world.

THE STREET DOGS OF THE PLANT WORLD

What is it with Philodendrons? They have to be the street dogs of the plant world. I don't feed them or water them, but they survive. I don't even remember where I got any of them.

Seriously, how do these viney, shiny houseplants exist? The books say their aerial roots hold to "most coarse surfaces." That must mean that as long as they can cling to a cement-like surface, they can live off of thin air.

But the many little and big Philodendrons that punctuate my house don't cling. They just dangle in thin air and when the dangling gets to be dangerous, I start wrapping them in and around themselves. When I and they were younger, I would put nails in the ceiling or the wall or around a window and try to create a jungle atmosphere. Lots of older graduate students like that effect.

I had one type of Philodendron (there are over 200 species) hanging at a window over the toilet in a bathroom. Every time my father came to visit, he insisted the thing kept wrapping itself around his ahem and interfered with his daily crossword puzzling. Let it be said that my father was definitely a coarse surface, the kind of man that is "hard to live with" when he is younger and becomes "a character" or "He threw the mold away" type as he gets older.

The Monstera is a Philodendron. You know that plant---huge with massive, split, glossy, leathery leaves. It has the eccentric habit of throwing off from its stem long (I measured one at 6 feet), buff-colored whips for, who knows, air, intimidation? I gave that monster to my daughter, Kathy. She has since given it to her brother Blake. It lives in Maine.

It arrived twenty-four years ago in our apartment dining room. When we moved to our Victorian, it kept growing at such a rate that for twelve years it had its own bathroom. I didn't encourage it. I watered it every month or two and would saw off a whip if it tried to sneak into the hall.

Then why do I keep Philodendrons if I don't particularly like them? Because I want greenery inside my house and leaf for leaf and, over the years, pound for pound there's not a better buy on the planet.

Get a 2" or 6" or 8" philodendron. Or you could just get a glass of water. Plop in the little vine and you've got a plant for life. Name me another plant that is so happy you got it that it will perform year in and year out, in sun and out of sun, with water or without water, with soil or without soil. Just name one.

God definitely threw away the mold when He made these characters.

IN PRAISE OF BLUEBERRIES

When we bought our home years ago, there were three blueberry bushes right in the middle of a great expanse of lawn. My husband wanted to take them out so he could mow in straight lines. I insisted on the wonder of blueberry desserts from our own side yard.

The first year I watched the tiny white flowers gradually turn into hard, urgent, green kernels that ripened into semi-sweet blue blueberries. A friend said they weren't really blueberries. They were huckleberries. My mother insisted they were whortleberries. I went to the books and found that there are three more names for the small fruit called "blueberry": hurtleberry, blaeberry and bilberry.

All of these names are interchangeable for the blue berries of the Vaccinium genus. Though each specie has a variation, New Englanders call them what most of the country calls them---blueberries. The huckleberries of the Plains States are wild and have ten little nutlets inside them that distinguish them from the normal blueberries.

Then there are the tiny Maine blueberries. PICKING blueberries is what most of us do. But in Maine you don't PICK blueberries, you RAKE blueberries. Yes. With a steel hand-held rake. The bushes are not in front of you. They crawl over the ground in a close tangle of tiny twigs, minute leaves and teeny berries. Getting those Maine blueberries is back-bending, leg-braking, hand-blackening WORK. The migrant workers I've talked to in Down East Maine have numerous cuts and scratches on their berry-stained hands and arms.

In their wild state blueberries can grow anyplace. They are found from Alaska to Florida, on all the continents and they have even been known to survive the winters above the Arctic Circle!

To cultivate blueberries, plant them in the fall or the spring. Their ideal condition is a moisture-retentive, acid soil. But they will yield in loose, sandy soil with the help of a nitrogen source such as ammonium sulfate. They prefer sun but will produce in the shade. If you have no room for them in your yard, blueberries will grow in deck containers filled with acid or peat-based soil. As you can see, these little berries will grow and produce anywhere!

Back to my three blueberry bushes. Now only ONE blueberry bush interrupts our lawn. The other two were relentlessly mowed down by the Deere.

Nonetheless, I have developed a fondness for blueberry desserts made from the high-piled, cellophane-topped, rubber-band-wrapped supermarket variety. One of my favorites is Blueberry Flummery---a rich, thick, blue-back decoction of the berries studded with a dollop of smooth, white sour cream. That recipe is one of the few "keepers" from a year-long foray into medieval cooking. I, also, combine fresh blueberries with sour cream and powdered sugar. Yum!

The Indians found the blueberry a better staple than the strawberry. They cooked them in with their meats and stews and dried them for winter stores. Nowadays and for many decades we have put them in and on everything: pancakes, muffins, waffles, pies, breads, shortcakes, tarts, puddings, turnovers, soups, jellies, sauces, relishes and even cheeses.

More than a century ago Oliver Wendell Holmes remarked that he was "amazed there should be a region of the earth where blueberry cake was not known." With its hardiness, productivity and casual temperament, the little blueberry has circled the globe.

Next year I'm having all the blueberries I want right in my own yard. Last week I traded my husband

Steve a tangle of raspberry canes that he abhorred for twenty prim and controlled blueberry bushes. They're on a sunny bank, my Berry Bank, surrounded by wood chips---husband and Deere-proof.

BLUEBERRY FLUMMERY RECIPE

2 cups fresh blueberries
1 cup water
1/4 cup cornstarch
1/4 cup sugar
1/8 tsp. salt
Juice of 1/2 a lemon
1 cup fresh blueberries
Sour cream
Optional: fresh mint leaves, chopped

Simmer the 2 cups blueberries and the water for 10 minutes over medium-high heat. Press the mixture through a sieve. Add enough water to the sieved juices to make 2 1/2 cups of juice. Mix together the cornstarch, sugar and salt. Add them to the blueberry juice. Cook over medium-low heat. Whisk until the sauce becomes thick and clear. Add the lemon juice. Cool. Chill in the refrigerator. When chilled, stir in the fresh blueberries and the mint. Serve in small, clear dessert bowls. Top with a dollop of sour cream. Serves 4-6 people.

HOW TO MAKE HERB AND BERRY VINEGARS

Find a beautiful bottle or jar.
Wash well.
Fill with WHITE vinegar.
Insert some sprigs of herb or some berries (8-12).
Cap, cork or wax over the bottle or jar.
Allow to "steep" for several weeks or months.
Keeps indefinitely or until herbs and berries get tired.
These vinegars are wonderful over any salad requiring vinegar.

BEST HERBS TO USE FOR YOUR VINEGARS

Rosemary
Thyme
Dill
Mint
Chive (Use chive spears and the stems with the chive flowers.)
Tarragon

BEST BERRIES TO USE FOR YOUR BERRY VINEGARS

Red Raspberries
Blueberries
Blackberries

NASTURTIUM VINEGAR

Pack a wide-mouthed jar, like a Mason jar, with nasturtium blossoms. Pour a good CIDER vinegar over the blossoms. Seal well and use it in your kitchen or pantry as a decoration. After it has set for several weeks, use it as a peppery-flavored vinegar over salads or wild greens.

Note: For a visual and nutritional treat, place nasturtium blossoms in the bottom of a pan or dish. Pour lemon or lime Jell-o over them. Refrigerate until set. Serve as a special dessert for your family and friends. Visually, it's gorgeous!

A FEW FLORAL FACTS ABOUT A FEW STATES

CALIFORNIA

California's name comes from that of an imaginary island in a 1510 romance by Ordonez de Montalvo. "California" was the name applied in the 1500's to all of the unknown and unexplored American northwest. Three hundred years later in 1848 gold was discovered in the millrace of John Sutter and from then on California was definitely on the known map. San Francisco went from a hamlet of several hundred people to a city of 20,000 in just three months.

But if it is gardener's gold you're seeking, those old gold mining camps are the place to go to find roses. Real roses, the old roses that the hybridizers have not tinkered with, the old roses that still smell. As millions of ounces of gold bullion left California, dozens of species of roses were planted there by the newly rich.

Most do not think of California as Rose Country, but their famous Rose Bowl Parade and Celebration of Old Roses Week attest to the enduring horticultural legacy of the Forty Niners. Visit some of those old mining camps found on any California map. Smell the roses and gather some for this old recipe:

To Make Conserve of Red Roses

Take one pound of red Rose-Buds and Bruise them with a Wooden Pestle in a Marble Mortar, adding by Degrees, of white Loaf-Sugar powdered and sifted, three pounds: continue beating them, till no Particles of the Roses can be seen, and till the Mass is all alike.

From a 1744 London cookbook <u>Adam's Luxury and Eve's Cookery</u>

"I left my heart in San Francisco."
Written by George Corry & Douglas Cross
Signature song of Tony Bennett (1962)

WYOMING

Wyoming, in the heart of the Rocky Mountains, is named for the Wyoming valley far away in Pennsylvania. The Wyoming valley in Penn's Woods is famous for a massacre of frontiersmen by Tory Rangers and their Mohawk allies in July of 1778. Over 100 years later Wyoming was admitted into the Union as the 44th state. Obviously, when it came to naming the state, there were some well-connected residents with family ties to that Pennsylvania Massacre.

But try to transplant some of Wyoming's gorgeous wildflowers east of the Mississippi and you'll have a time of it. The Lewisia and Clarkia flowers (so named for Lewis and Clark whose Expedition did NOT enter Wyoming) often wither and die back East. Every year the Erythronium will push through the last 3" of hard snow to bloom on time in the Rockies, but it often dwindles to nothing after several years in a cultivated garden. Wild Erigonums and Mariposas spurn our sanctuaries of civilization.

But we have harnessed one of their prize plants, Aquilegia, the Columbine. It is garden-broken all over the East and is as much a herald of Spring as were the pioneers who year after year plodded through Wyoming following the Oregon Trail, the Overland Trail and the Bozeman Trail through those fields of native wildflowers.

"Down in the canyon cottonwood whispers
A Song of Wyoming for me."
Written and Sung by John Denver

145

VIRGINIA

During the earliest period of American history, the name "Virginia" embraced all of North America not secured by France or Spain. Sir Walter Raleigh (of the cloak incident) staked claims to the New World in 1584 for his paramour, the "Virgin" Queen Elizabeth. But Virginia languished until Captain John Smith and his band of convicts and indentured servants, a rough bunch, established the first colony in America at Jamestown in 1607. These raucous men were a far cry from the genteel image of modern-day Virginians. Captain Smith had such a time getting them to actually work that he put a sign--"No Work. No Eat"-- over the gates in Jamestown. The Captain must have succeeded because somebody planted a field of wheat within two weeks of landing and within several years an early journal records that " a garden was laid off and the seeds of fruit and vegetables <u>not</u> indigenous" were sown.

But the real growth and wealth of Virginia came from an indigenous plant, tobacco. The Indians loved it and so did the Europeans. By 1689 the annual export of tobacco exceeded 15 million pounds. And from tobacco came the money to build the extensive plantations and with them the noble gardens of Virginia. Some of these grand estates still exist bearing their romantic names proudly in the tobacco-flavored air: Claremont Manor, Rock Castle, Poplar Hall, Flower de Hundred.

"Carry me back to old Virginny."
Written by African American minstrel James Bland
The State Song of Virginia

MAINE

Maine's poor soil and brief growing season have confined agriculture to local needs, but she is the unlikely birthplace of the first "pleasure garden" in America. A map drawn up by Champlain in 1604 shows a small but beautiful garden in the short-lived settlement of what is now Neutral Island in the St. Croix River between Maine and New Brunswick.

Maine is the only state whose state flower is NOT a flower. The state "flower" of Maine is the White Pine Cone and Tassel (Pinus strobos, linnaeus).

When Chicago hosted the 1893 World's Fair, states were asked to choose and present their state flowers. There were three options on the ballot in Maine for state flower: the goldenrod, the apple blossom and the pine cone and tassel. Out of 17,000 votes cast, the pine cone and tassel received 10,000 votes. So there you go! The pine cone and, don't forget, the tassel has been and still is Maine's state flower. After all, 90% of the state is forested. It is nicknamed The Pine Tree State.

In the Spring Maine's main export is one of the tastiest wild forest foods: the fiddlehead of the Ostrich fern. If you have never tasted this luscious, delicate vegetable, get some next Spring and boil them. Throw off the first water. Re-boil. When fork-tender, slather with butter, salt and pepper. The taste is between a green bean, an asparagus and an artichoke.

Many writers and artists live hidden among the crags and boulders of Maine's coastline.

My son Blake, his wife Carrie, daughter Avonlea and son Jack intend to plant a vegetable and flower garden in the cold soil beside their warm parsonage there in Southwest Harbor on Mt. Desert Island.

Katherine White, wife of E.B. White, wrote wonderful garden stories for the New Yorker in the 50's and 60's.

Her book <u>Onward and Upward In The Garden</u> attests to the Yankee ingenuity one must have to garden in this cold, densely pine-coned and tasseled state.

<u>Discovering Old Bar Harbor and Acadia National Park:</u>
<u>An Unconventional History and Guide</u>
by Ruth Ann Hill

LOUISIANA

Louisiana was named by the Frenchman La Salle (1682) for Louis XIV and became a French colony in 1731. When one thinks of Louisiana, one thinks of New Orleans, Mardi Gras and the Bayou which are all part of the state's French heritage.

Louisiana burst on the culinary scene with its Cajun cooking and blackened fishes. "Cajun" is a relatively recent appellation designating those persons on the gulf coast who are of mixed White, Indian and Black blood. From that mixture has come a new way of cooking and a new international cuisine.

But let's talk Blackberry pie. It's my favorite pie. Blackberry pie is a state staple. B. M. Young of Morgan City, La. has developed one of the best of the new breeds of blackberries, the Youngberry. This member of the Rose family (you can tell by its bloom) was a weed to be destroyed to the early colonists.

Man has been eating blackberries forever. Aeschylus and Hippocrates mention them 500 years before Christ. They are a palliative for high blood pressure and provide heavy potassium and little sodium.

But Blackberry pie: 4 cups fresh blackberries. Mix in 1 cup sugar, 1/3 cup flour, 1/2 tsp. cinnamon. Dot with lots of butter. Cover with a top crust. Slit the crust. Bake at 425 for 35-45 minutes until the crust is browned and the lovely purple juice begins to bubble out of the slits. Serve warm. Or you can top a slice with cheese, whipped cream or ice cream. I like it warm, unadorned. But Blackberry pie. Served warm on a hot Bayou night when the bugs are biting and the moon is low...

In French "Mardi Gras" means "Fat Tuesday."
It is the day before Ash
Wednesday when the Lenten Fast begins.

TEXAS

It's big. Edna Ferber called it "Giant." Yet Texas was largely unsettled until a hundred years ago when stock raising became its leading industry. It's named, like so many of our states, after the Indians, the Tejas. La Salle dabbled there in 1685 (he was ubiquitous). The Spanish Franciscans set up a mission and a few settlements in 1690. Before that in the 1500's, Cortez, de Vaca and Coronado walked through on their way to the El Dorado of the Aztecs farther south.

For centuries they had all walked on and over that good old black gold---oil, petroleum, Texas tea. It wasn't until the early 1900's that all that black stuff oozing out of the ground, all those hydrocarbons from decayed and compressed plants transformed Texas into an urban and industrial domain which produces about 23% of the nation's mineral output and is first in oil production.

Texas is, of course, known for its miles and miles of Texas bluebonnets (lupines), the Alamo and its--- bigness. Its bigness and starry, starry nights where a big handful of stars can be plucked from the low, black heavens and thrown into the face of the 49 little states to the north.

"The eyes of Texas are upon you all the
live long day."
Written by John Lang Sinclair
Sung to the tune of "I've Been Working On The
Railroad"

KENTUCKY

The feud between the Hatfields and the McCoys originated in this state. In the early 1800's Kentucky was primarily a state of small farms that had little use for slave labor. But after 1840, as a trading region along the banks of the Ohio, it became a huge slave market for the lower South. But it was always a border state on the Slavery Issue. When the Civil War started, some 30,000 Kentuckians fought for the Confederacy and twice that number for the Union. With neighbor literally against neighbor, the end of the War did not bring the end of hostilities. The Kentucky Split expressed itself not only politically but in industrial disputes and in the family feuds of the Cumberland Hatfields and McCoys.

One thing no one has ever disputed is that the 8,000 square miles of east central Kentucky known as the Bluegrass Region is one of the most fertile and prosperous sections of the state. If you want a grass that is gracefully aristocratic, deep green, strongly recuperative, widely adaptable, easily cared for and considered the best sod former, get Kentucky blue grass seed. For improving your own established lawn, sow 2-3 lbs. per 1,000 square feet. Fertilize to provide 3 lbs. or more of nitrogen per 1,000 square feet annually for good, deep color. Yes, Kentucky blue grass does have a bluish hue.

In Kentucky the world-famous horse farms have grown up around the three feet high pastures of Kentucky blue grass. Citation and Man 0' War battled to the finish lines at the renowned Kentucky Derby fortified with the nutrients from this wonder grass.

Daniel Boone, the blazer of the Wilderness Road over which the pioneers moved west, was known to shoot a few into the air as a salute every time he came home to Kentucky and its waving fields of blue.

"The sun shines bright in the old Kentucky home."
Written by Stephen Foster
The State Song Of Kentucky

CONNECTICUT

"Connecticut" means "long river place." The Algonquins contributed the name and the Connecticut River gave the definition. The river begins in the lakes of northern New Hampshire, forms a natural boundary between Vermont and New Hampshire, flows south through Massachusetts and Connecticut and ends its 407 mile journey in Long Island Sound.

Not because of this famous river but because of its fabulous climate is Connecticut the best possible place to have a traditional English perennial border. That coveted border is usually about 100 ft. long and 8-10 ft. wide.

It's nice if you can have background shrubs, but if not, be sure to include stands of peonies, bearded irises and day lilies as a foundation for your border. Spring Oriental poppies, summer phloxes and fall asters are great. Dig in some white baby's breath, some plates of yellow achillea, a few old hollyhocks, some invasive oenothera and filipendula rubra, and astilbe, and veronica and all kinds of campanula, and epimedium, and cimicifuga, yes, and monarda for the bees, and dicentras for the spring, and, oh, columbines, and did I say delphiniums?, and liatrises, yes for the pointiness, and the wonderful cones of the echinachea, and, a must, black-eyed Susans, and the golden-eyed Shastas, and chrysanthemums for eating, and, and...I could go on for 407 pages. See why Connecticut is the ideal place to garden?

<u>A Connecticut Yankee In King Arthur's Court</u>
by Mark Twain

USA FLOWER CONTRIBUTIONS TO THE GARDENS OF THE WORLD

Phlox
Butterfly Weed (Asclepias)
Cleome
Liatris
Lupine
Hibiscus
Coreopsis
California Poppy
Gaillardia
Echinacea (Cone Flower)
Physostegia (Obedient Plant)
Black-eyed Susans
Yucca
Canna Lily
Tradescantia
Wild Indigo
Wild Hyacinth
Wild Leek
Wild Geranium
Indian Paintbrush
Lobelia (Cardinal Flower)
Joe Pye Weed
Gentia
Helianthus (Sun Flower)
Solidago (Goldenrod)
Polemonium (Jacob's Ladder)
Lysimachia (Gooseneck Strife)
Anemone
Iris

ROBINSON CRUSOE AND MONA LISA

Think about it. Daniel Defoe really doesn't get much credit. He wrote <u>Robinson Crusoe</u> in 1719. The book has been such a success that it's never been out of print since then. Almost three hundred years of non-stop publishing should be enough for people to talk about him nowadays. But you never hear, "Wow, I just read Defoe again. What a guy!" No, you never hear anyone, even in the ivory towers of universities, say that. Plus Defoe wrote <u>Moll Flanders.</u> Those two novels were really one of the first attempts at novel writing. Until then, stories were written in drama or poetry. You never hear anyone say, "I just finished so and so's new novel. It was great. I'm so happy Defoe started that genre, aren't you?" No, you don't hear those things.

You do hear, "If necessity is the mother of invention, she is never more pregnant than with me." You do hear adages like that denoting need wedded to invention. That's just how Defoe started writing. He was bankrupt. He had seven children and a wife. He needed money. In the same year of 1705 a crazy young Scotsman by the name of Alexander Selkirk was in trouble half a world away. He had swashbuckled his way around the Pacific for a couple of years. He was a member of a crew that had scurvy, was gangrenous and was not happy. Their ship was slowly being eaten by worms. The captain was desperately trying to get back to England. In South America, young Selkirk decided he wanted off. (Another version has him forcibly removed from the ship.) He was deposited on a spit of land miles off the coast of Chile.

Believe it or not, he survived by himself for four years on that tiny island. When he was rescued, his story brought him fame and fortune. All England read about him. Defoe read about him and thought,

"Maybe, just maybe, I could write his story and get out of debt." He did write the story, but he couldn't find a publisher. He sold his manuscript about a man named Robinson Crusoe who is marooned for 27 years on an island in the Caribbean for just 10 pounds. The public loved his book. It was an instant best seller. But he had sold it for only 10 pounds. He was famous, but still penniless.

That little island where the original Robinson Crusoe, Selkirk, was abandoned is now called Isla Robinson Crusoe. It is home to the rarest plant in the world, Dendroseris neriifolia. What makes this plant the rarest in the world is that there is only one known specimen living in the wild. Dendroseris neriifolia is a droopy tree with elongated leaves and tiny pale yellow flowers. I'm sure Selkirk never imagined that his island prison would ever be the home of the rarest plant in the world. I'm positive he never imagined that he would have a whole island named after his ordeal and that he would be the inspiration for one of the first novels. Truth is stranger than fiction.

What if I told you that an edible bulb the size of a small onion once sold for the price of a house. You probably wouldn't believe me. It's true. There was an insane period in Dutch history between 1633 and 1637 called Tulipomania. Think of that four-year period in Holland as you would the last four years of the twentieth century in America when sane middle-aged men and women went cuckoo with Internet stocks. The Dutch could buy two tons of butter or one tulip bulb. They bought the bulb. Americans could buy a vacation house or put their money in companies that had never earned one penny. They put their money in companies that had never earned one penny. There are quirky periods of fiscal insanity in the history of the world.

Tulips are one of the most beautiful of all flowers. Holland is still known for these kingly blooms. We have hybridized them into frayed parrot shapes and into all colors of the rainbow and streaks in between. I once won a blue ribbon at a flower show by just standing one dozen pale pink perfect tulips in a tall antique silver and crystal relish dish. They looked---priceless.

In the spring a bed of tulips can take your breath away. They originated in the barren, wind-scraped steppes of central Asia and migrated via the Turks to Europe in the 1500's. The Dutch in particular loved them. Mike Dash has written a book about their irrational love affair with the tulip: <u>Tulipomania: The Story of the World's Most Coveted Flower and the Extraordinary Passions It Aroused.</u> In it he tells the story of a small tavern owner Wouter Winkel who died in 1633 leaving his seven children destitute. But it was 1633 and that was the beginning of Tulip Fever. His children dug up his bed of tulips, sold them at auction and became very wealthy. Tulipomania ended with the financial collapse of the market. People went bankrupt and the whole of Holland was befuddled by their collective bout of insanity.

But it is not insane to love, to care for and to watch flowers. Yes, watch flowers. In 1970 in Java 34,000 people came to watch the bloom of one of the world's largest and certainly the world's smelliest flower, Titan arum. People held handkerchiefs to their noses as they gazed at the pale green and orchid spathe from which had emerged a giant, six foot, phallus-like "flower." These manly structures can grow to 12 ft tall. Two blooms of the "Penis Plant," as it was called, occurred within two years in New York prompting the Bronx to designate the giant arum its official flower! The University of Wisconsin has had several "Corpse Flowers" (it's smelly) bloom. In 2001 30,000 people came to watch one bloom. Another bloomed in 2002 but collapsed several days later under its own phallic weight.

But why the awful odor? The putrid, corpse-like smell attracts carrion beetles in its homeland of Sumatra. The beetles in turn pollinate the plant. This stinky, risque rarity was the talk of Seattle not too long ago. Another Corpse Flower was about to bloom! Thousands turned out to watch. A scientist at the University of Washington botany greenhouse rhapsodized, "It feels so much like when my two boys were born." So, there you go. People not only buy plants for irrational amounts of money, they, also, say things about plants that are totally absurd.

Let's go from the ridiculous to the sublime. There is a flower called the Holy Spirit, Espiritu Santo. It is one of the rarest and most beautiful of all flowers. In its cup is the daintiest figure of a dove, pure and white as the snow. It grows in California and in Central America.

California is a flower paradise. 30% of the plants in the Golden State occur naturally no where else. In the Northeast of the United States 13% of the plants occur naturally no where else, and in the British Isles only 1% occur naturally no where else. So California is a charmed place in more ways than one.

There are charmed plants. Four-leaf clovers are lucky. Everyone knows that. As a child in Ohio and occasionally as an adult, I have searched through the grass for a four-leaf clover. Remember the song, "I'm looking over/ A four-leaf clover?" Well, what kind of a song should we sing to Park Farland? June 16, 1975 he found a 14-leaf clover near Sioux City, South Dakota! And Paul Haizlip found another 14-leaf clover in Bellevue, Washington on June 22, 1987.

What are the odds here?

When you are searching through the grass for a 4 or 14-leaf clover, you see lots of weeds. Most of them are small and hug the ground. They resist sprays and lawn doctors. They are pests you learn to live around. Most of the time, unless you are very fussy, you don't notice them.

But imagine the mind-set of the person who first introduced Heracleum mantegazzianum into the American soil. "The Americans will love this plant. It's big like their country." Its common name came to be Giant Hogweed. See the "weed" in there? It's the Largest Weed In The World. When it was brought to America, it was sold as a nice ornamental plant. Who could possibly think that a plant that is 12 feet high with 36 inch leaves could ever be regarded as anything but unwieldy and, yes, weedy?

I can imagine the first people who grew this transplant from Russia. It took over the entire back of their gardens. And the next year there were four of them. Weeds multiply. They could with difficulty be cut down, but they couldn't be dug up. I guess those first people who bought and grew the Giant Hogweed just had to sell their homes in the dead of winter and move on. Let's find out who first introduced this plant to us and find out what nursery sold it and who the first buyers were and……

The Largest Flower in the world is not the Corpse Plant aka Penis Plant but the Rafflesia. You have to go all the way to Borneo to see it. Even then, you have to go up into the tropical forest, hack your way through lots of plant material and crawl around in the dense underbrush. Your chances of finding one are pretty slim. Rafflesia is not only the largest flower but it is one of the rarest. It measures up to 3 1/2 feet in diameter. Amazingly, it has no leaf, no stem and no root! It just presides. It takes nine months to grow but deteriorates in just 10 days. I've seen pictures of them---massive, orange, with scalloped edges and a huge round center that looks like a small pond.

The Lord sure has a sense of humor. When He created you and me and every thing, He spoke into reality not only beauty, variety, detail and infinity, but He tinged it all with a big Mona-Lisa smile. That's how I think of it anyway.

NO MORE RED SALVIA!

It's April or May. Look around. All of the garden centers, supermarkets and sundries stores are sporting acres of "bedding" plants. There do exist breath-taking, interesting, striking annuals, but for some unknown reason the growers have confined themselves decade after decade to petunias, marigolds, ageratum, coleus and red salvia!

Given a choice, who really wants these flowers? Yes, they are reliable. Yes, they are easy to grow. Yes, they are forgiving. But they are terrible for bouquets, hard on the eyes and terminally boring! Obviously, the growers think we love them, for they have spent years developing white ageratum, purple salvia, quadruple, striped petunias and combs and plumes in colors the Aztecs never intended.

Why all this scientific energy directed toward essentially banal plants? I blame the scientists just as I blame the designers for micro-minis and platform shoes.

In 1851 at Mockern in Saxony the first agriculture experimental station was established. A young American horticulture student named Samuel W. Johnson visited the site and was so impressed by the experiments in soil treatments, new farm crops and stock feeding and breeding that he returned to Connecticut and began calling for a similar facility. He became a professor at Yale and used the post to lobby the Connecticut legislature for $2,800 to start such an experiment at the Department of Chemistry at Wesleyan College in 1875. Later it was moved to New Haven, but Connecticut's station was so successful that other states soon set up their own facilities. The experimental stations eventually became the testing grounds for ornamental plants.

In England in the late nineteenth century the rage was mosaiculture or bedding-out. Neat, reliable flowers were required for this silly stage in horticulture. Flowers became clocks, faces, trains, buggies. Public parks and landscapes were sculpted with ageratums, verbenas, lobelias, geraniums, alyssums, begonias and the variegated leaves of the coleus and croton. It seems the testing stations in the 3rd millennium are still trying to perfect the same plants Johnson encouraged in 1875.

We don't need to spend another century on red salvia. There are plenty of other annuals that complement those of us who live in northern climes much better than all those sub-tropical plants.

Imagine an annual border lazily mingling the sky-blue cornflower, the giant, white, airy stems of the baby's breath, the pink and fuchsia daisies of the cosmos, ferny marguerite, the saucer-shaped flowers of the California poppy, the deep purple cups of the campanula, the big daisies of the Swan River and the dense blue spikes of the larkspur.

All of these annuals make a show. All are reliable. All are great for bouquets. Why don't we see acres of these each spring? They're more beautiful. They're more now. They're more---not red salvia.

When the public doesn't buy micro-minis and platform shoes, the designers stop making them. If we don't buy these traditional bedding plants they foist on us, the scientists and growers will get the message. It's been 150 years. Demand a change!

A PUMPKIN PAPER

In the 1950's Whittaker Chambers produced incriminating microfilm and papers probing Alger Hiss' unAmerican activities. He had kept the evidence hidden in the most American of all places---in a pumpkin shell. They have become known to history as "The Pumpkin Papers."

"Peter, Peter, Pumpkin Eater.
Had a wife and couldn't keep her.
Put her in a pumpkin shell
And there he kept her very well."

This may not be the sanest course for distraught husbands, but Chambers, that convert from Communism to Capitalism, conceived an ironic idea that came to symbolize the triumph of the American gourd over the Russian sickle.

The pumpkin is a gourd belonging to the Cucurbitaceae family as do melons, squash and cucumbers. In 1585 Sir Walter Raleigh's men found the Indians on Roanoke Island growing a huge vegetable that the Indians called "Macocgwer. We called them Pompions and they are very good." By the early 1600's the pumpkin was a staple for the settlers. The Indians had taught them how to stew it and stew it they did so often that it was called "New England Standing Dish." It was bland but life-sustaining.

The pumpkin would have gone the way of all "flesh" had it not been for the ingenious housewives who began to add a little of this and a little of that in order to improve the taste. The first recipe for Pumpkin Pie in the early 1700's calls for "one quart milk, I pint pompkin, 4 eggs, molasses, allspice and ginger in a crust, bake 1 hour." It was called Pumpkin Pudding.

The early puddings had crusts and were the same as our pies. The molasses used in all early pies was a cheap by-product of expensive West Indian sugar. It came in great hogsheads and was bought at the ubiquitous General Stores a gallon at a time.

Pumpkin pie has become the standard dessert at American tables of Thanksgiving. I love pumpkin pie, but I only make it once a year. It's that special. I use my mother's recipe which is a pumpkin chiffon-type pie with a delicate layer of custard on the bottom (caused by beating the egg whites separately and then folding them into the mixture). But I like the heavy, spiced brown pies favored by the early and modern Americans, too.

Pumpkin pie was so wedded to Thanksgiving that in Connecticut in the 17th century one town could not get the molasses needed for the pies in time for their Thanksgiving Day feasts. So they delayed the celebration of Thanksgiving until the molasses arrived. I understand. I wait 364 days for my pumpkin pie.

In the late fall I do make pumpkin bread often--- heavy, moist warm slices with creamy butter running off and oiling my hand. And pumpkin soup---tawny and salty sweet with a butter ball in the middle dissolving into tiny circles. And pumpkin custard---I make this a lot. And pumpkin ice cream---not one of my favorites, but a treat.

A bigger treat is to go out into the country where there are 500-acre farms with 50 acres devoted to these orange behemoths. It's an orange and brown fall day---hard sun, cool air. Thousands of pumpkins litter the earth. You know that they are members of the gourd family from their eccentric shapes. Not all pumpkins are round, jolly jack-o'lanterns. More than a few are tall rectangles like little apartment buildings. Some have big pumpkin warts and pimples. Others have deep, deep navels with strong, strong stems jutting out. They're all full of Vitamin A, seeds for drying and winter-by-the-fire-eating and flesh for soups and tarts and custards and pumpkin pies. Surveying the green and orange-dotted field, you know why the first European transplants were so grateful—so much is in so much.

Seventeenth century colonists recited a bit of doggerel that reflected their gratitude for, if not their culinary delight in, the prolific gourd:

"For pottage and puddings and custards and pies,
Our pumpkins and turnips are common supplies.
We have pumpkins at morning and pumpkins at noon;
If it were not for pumpkins, we should be undoon."

The Pumpkin Papers may have "undoon" Alger Hiss, but the pumpkin and its products have and will festoon American tables and taste buds from the First Thanksgiving until....

NARANGA

When I was a little girl, every Christmas Eve my mother gave my sister and me an orange before we went to bed. We played with it, smelled its skin and finally ate this very rare winter treat. Today we can have oranges every eve December through November.

The orange appears to have originated in southeast Asia, China and India. By 4000 B.C. it was well established. The word "orange" comes from a Sanskrit word "naranga." So probably the Indians were the first to cultivate it, but it was the Chinese who bred the orange from a bitter citrus into a sweet fruit.

Until the 16th century very few people in Europe had ever tasted an orange. The orange ball was, of course, legendary in the Old World. Explorers and travelers had told tales of its delicious taste and smell for hundreds of years. Even though they had brought back seeds of the fruit from the Orient, the harsh climate of Europe killed all the infant trees. For Citrus sinensis can only be grown in sub-tropical and tropical countries.

How to grow these prized fruits in a hostile environment? In 16th century Europe glass making burst forth on a grand scale. Glass-enclosed spaces were created. They were called orangeries. Orangeries were among the first greenhouses. Now Europe could have oranges. They could plant the precious seeds from India and China and nurture the fledgling trees in a controlled environment.

In the United States commercial production of oranges is only in Zone 9B which encompasses California, the Rio Grande valley in Texas, southern Arizona, southern Louisiana and, of course, Florida. The United States and our southern neighbor, Brazil, account for more than two-thirds of all oranges produced in the world.

Oranges, like people, come in all shapes and sizes. Most of us probably prefer the Navel orange that was developed in California and Florida. The skin is thick and easy to peel. The inside is seedless and those firm segments just peel away to release their succulence and sweetness with every bite. Ironically, the Navel orange is the ONLY orange whose juice is NEVER used for orange juice because it turns bitter when exposed to air!

Florida is synonymous with Oranges and Orange Juice. The orange blossom is its state flower. Big orange oranges with green leaves adorn Florida license plates and everybody buys Fresh-Squeezed Orange Juice for everyday use at the nearest Publix's.

The thin-skinned Valencia and Pineapple oranges of Florida produce the best orange juice. Most growers would favor the Valencia. It is usually seedless. The very seedy Pineapple orange has a good color and taste and is the leading midseason commercial orange.

Those who live in Florida often prefer the Temple oranges. They have a very rich flavor. In Season you often see the Snow Birds sucking on this cross between a Mandarin and an orange. They can't get those Temples up North.

Israel has given us the Jaffa orange. It is usually seedless and a good all-purpose orange with a slightly tart taste. The Seville orange from the Mediterranean makes the best orange marmalade, some say.

When I was young, every once in a long while my mother would get Blood oranges from Spain. Before citrus growers started forwarding their fruits northward, any orange was a find. These Blood oranges were good, but the dramatic, dark vermilion, bloody streaks were off-putting as was, of course, the very name—BLOOD oranges!

The Mandarin orange from California is confined to the little cans of Mandarin oranges on store shelves that are, as far as I can determine, used exclusively in a retro dish called Ambrosia. Unlike the common sweet orange, the rind of the Mandarin orange is a brilliant emerald green when ripe. Florida and California grow Mandarins but canneries buy up most of the crop. According to those who have eaten them fresh, they are delicious.

Then in 1982 Clementines arrived on American shores in those little wooden crates with plastic netting over them. Most people think of these Christmas treats as little tangerines. They are not. They are the smallest variety of the Mandarin orange. Imported mainly from Spain and Morocco, Clementines are a cross between a Chinese Mandarin and a sweet orange. Small, usually seedless and very sweet, they are beloved by children. They are called Clementines after an Algerian monk, Clement, who was tending his mandarin oranges, saw a mutant, fostered it and soon his trees were producing little Clementinos.

Whether the orange is big or small, a gauge of its juiciness is how heavy it feels in your hand. Try to find the oranges that are shiny, but the ugly truth is that supermarket oranges have usually been "de-greened" (ripened) with ethylene gas. They are then washed with a detergent, colored with orange dye, coated with wax and stored for long periods of time before shipping. Tree-ripened oranges are rare in the markets. It is the cooler temperatures that turn the oranges from green to orange and growers can't wait to get their produce to market.

Another ugly truth is that the Vitamin C in an orange is so scant that you would have to eat bushels of them to get the benefit. Oranges, however, lower cholesterol and assist in the digestion of food high in fat.

Citrus was important in the prevention of scurvy during long sea voyages in the Age of Exploration and Discovery. Those early explorers took citrus seeds with them from the orangeries of Europe and planted the orange all over the New World. In most places the climate was not conducive to orange trees and the seeds did not germinate. But Ponce de Leon gave thousands of citrus seeds to his men in 1513. Wherever they went, they were instructed to plant those seeds.

What did Ponce de Leon discover?

The Fountain of Youth. Remember?

And where is that Fountain and where did Ponce de Leon and all his men scatter those orange seeds?

In FLORIDA!

All of us naranga fans thank you, Senor Ponce!

THE EAST SIDE OF EDEN

"Now the Lord God had planted a garden in the east, in Eden, and there he put the man he had formed. And the Lord God made all kinds of trees grow out of the ground---trees that were pleasing to the eye and good for food. In the middle of the garden were the tree of life and the tree of the knowledge of good and evil. A river watering the garden flowed from Eden, from there it was separated into four headwaters. The name of the first is the Pishon; it winds through the entire land of Havilah where there is gold. (The gold of that land is good; aromatic resin and onyx are also there.) The name of the second is Gihon. It winds through the entire land of Cush. The name of the third river is the Tigris. It runs along the east side of Asshur. And the fourth river is the Euphrates." Genesis 2: 8-14

The two most famous gardens and two of the most famous couples in the entire history of the world were located in modern-day Iraq.

The most famous garden, the one it all harks back to, is the Garden of Eden. The historic site for the Garden of Eden is a town 196 miles southwest of Baghdad called Abu Shah Rain. In ancient times it was called Eridu.

Archaeologists have been digging at Eridu for over 100 years. What fascinates them about this particular site is that civilization can be traced back to 5,000 B.C. there.

Civilization is not the same thing as habitation. Civilization implies a settled community with an organized structure and a record-keeping capacity. Habitation is a term which means just lived there, sojourned there.

Even though Eridu is a fascinating dig and should and will be pursued by archaeologists interested in the origins of civilization, the Bible doesn't place the Garden of Eden at Eridu. If you trace the paths of the four river boundaries of Eden, it was quite a capacious garden extending from modern-day Iraq over to Turkey and down to Ethiopia. So the Bible defines the original garden as a landmass rather than a mass of land.

It is interesting that the word "garden" is used in the Bible for the terrain surrounding Iraq. Obviously the climate has changed since then. The Bible says all kinds of trees that were "pleasing to the eye and good for food" grew there in Eden land. But for at least the last 5,000 years, most of the terrain around the Euphrates has been desert and inhospitable to grass, trees and flowers.

That was the problem for Amytis. Here she was in a political marriage to crazy Nebuchadnezzar. She had made the journey all the way from her lush, green, mountainous homeland to Babylon, to here, to the unforgiving sun, to the very dry, boring, monotonous, flat desert. And because she was the daughter of the King of the Medes, she had to stay there---all her life! Oh, how Amytis complained, "It's so boring and flat here, Nebuchadnezzar! From the palace turrets as far as the eye can see, there is not a drop of green! I'm so homesick, Nebuchadnezzar!"

Now Nebuchadnezzar was not just any ordinary king. He was king of kings in the world of 600 B.C. In bloody wars he had conquered all the lands in the Middle and Near East. He had even besieged Jerusalem and taken a lot of the treasures from Solomon's Temple dedicated to the one true God back to Babylon and put them "in the treasure house of his god." (Daniel 1:2)

In addition, "(Nebuchadnezzar) had ordered Ashpenaz, chief of his court officials, to bring (back to Babylon) some of the Israelites from the royal family and the nobility---young men without any physical defect, handsome, showing aptitude for every kind of learning, well informed, quick to understand, and qualified to serve in the king's palace. (Ashpenaz) was to teach them the language and literature of the Babylonians. The king assigned them a daily amount of food and wine from the king's table. They were to be trained for three years and after that, they were to enter the king's service. Among these were some from Judah: Daniel..." Daniel 1: 3-6

So Hebrew Daniel, famous for the Lion's Den, and Median Amytis were both in a sense captives of Babylonian Nebuchadnezzar. Queen Amytis was stuck in a politically arranged marriage far from her homeland and Daniel was a prisoner of war who had been hiked all the way to Babylon to be trained for service in the king's palace. It was a life sentence for both of them.

But these two captives became very famous. As everyone knows, Daniel was so smart and so godly that he became Nebuchadnezzar's Prime Minister. (Daniel 2:48) And Amytis was the reason for the second most famous garden in history---The Hanging Gardens of Babylon.

"In addition to its size, Babylon surpasses in splendor any city in the world." So wrote the famous historian Herodotus in 450 B.C.

The city rose out of the desert like a giant candelabra. Babylon, first built by Hammurabi the great Law Giver in 1792 B.C., was at its apex 1,300 years later under Nebuchadnezzar. The giant, desert metropolis was filled with libraries and with men who were versed in medicine, alchemy, botany, zoology, chemistry, astronomy and math. Their system of numbers was not based like ours on a base of 10, but on a base of 60. They had already divided the day into 24 hours of 60 minutes with each minute composed of 60 seconds. These were not backward, nomadic tribesmen. Except for the boring terrain, Amytis and Daniel had been transported to a much more stimulating and erudite environment than either Media or Jerusalem.

Nebuchadnezzar had rebuilt and fashioned Babylon into the most magnificent city of its time. Why not, he thought, build for dear and complaining Amytis a mountain of greenery right here in the desert. He knew he had access to the brains and the manpower to do the task. So one fine desert day the king of kings said to his queen of queens, "Amytis, my dear, if the mountain won't come to Nebuchadnezzar, Nebuchadnezzar will build the mountain."

And that is sort of how the Hanging Gardens of Babylon came to be. They were and have been considered so unique and unparalleled that they are one of the Seven Wonders of the Ancient World.

The ancient texts say the garden was composed mainly of trees. It was 400 ft. wide, 400 ft. long and as much as 320 ft. high. At over twice the height of the Statue of Liberty, this was a massive mountain of greenery. Philo (20 B.C.---40 A.D.) says that the gardens are "a work of art of royal luxury and its most striking feature is that the labor of cultivation is suspended above the heads of the spectators."

Above the heads of the spectators? Until the Hanging Gardens, a garden was under you. You bent down, planted and cultivated it in good old terra firma. When you looked at your garden, you were looking down or over—not up. This garden was suspended in the air. In awe Philo continues: "It has plants cultivated above ground level and the roots of the trees are embedded in an upper terrace rather than in the earth." Who ever heard of massive trees whose roots were high up in the air?

There were tiers and tiers of trees and plants rising magically like a mirage in the desert. "It consists of vaulted terraces raised one above another and resting upon cube-shaped pillars. These (pillars) are hollow and filled with earth to allow trees of the largest size to be planted in them." (Strabo 63 B.C.---24 A.D.) These thickly planted trees and plants had "great size and other charms and gave pleasure to the beholder." (Diodorus Siculus 90---21 B.C.)

The Hanging Gardens of Babylon, though designed to please one homesick queen, became the major attraction for most of the world at that time. People came from all over to see Nebuchadnezzar's achievement. Learned engineers and historians flocked to Babylon to see this mountain of green in the tan desert and to learn how the Babylonians had designed and constructed such an earth-shaking structure.

"The platforms on which the garden stood consisted of huge slabs of stone covered with layers of reed, asphalt and tiles. Over this a covering with sheets of lead that the water which drenched through the earth might not rot the foundation. Upon all these was laid earth of a convenient depth sufficient for the growth of the greatest trees. When the soil was laid even and smooth, it was planted with all sorts of trees which both for greatness and beauty might delight the spectators," says Diodorus Siculus, the great Greek historian who wrote 40 volumes of history, <u>Bibliotheca Historica,</u> chronicling the beginning of Greek civilization through Alexander the Great's exploits down to Caesar's Gallic Wars.

Anyone who has ever gardened knows that plants need sunlight and water. In ancient Babylon sunlight was definitely not a problem. But water. No matter how many slaves Nebuchadnezzar had, there would never be enough of them to carry buckets of water continually from the Euphrates up to the Hanging Gardens. As Nebuchadnezzar had brought Amytis' greenery to Babylon, he would bring the waters of the Euphrates to his mountain. His engineers were so ingenious that even today scientists can't figure out exactly how they irrigated the Hanging Gardens.

Strabo says tantalizingly, "The ascent to the highest story is by stairs and at their side are water engines by means of which people appointed expressly for the purpose are continually employed in raising water from the Euphrates into the gardens." So we have stairs and parallel to them "water engines."

Diodorus says "the water machines raised the water in great abundance from the river although no one outside could see it." There are many theories about what these water engines were and how they worked.

Engineers have over the centuries made elaborate drawings of irrigation systems that would deliver the water from the River Euphrates over to the Hanging Gardens and then up, up, up all those levels to the trees and plants. They are interesting to study, but no consensus has been reached. How this huge mountain of suspended greenery was watered is as enigmatic as how another Wonder of the Ancient World, the Pyramid at Gizeh, was built. In the modern world we are very limited in our knowledge of the machinations of the ancient world.

One can presume, however, that Amytis was thrilled. One sees her awakening and gazing upon a veritable Eden of trees and plants. One imagines her taking her morning tea under a tamarind tree with soft tendrils of herbs cushioning her royal feet. One opines that she and Nebuchadnezzar (on one of his better days) are strolling up and down the stairs of the magical mountain as the apricot sun slides into the desert sands. One must consider Amytis happy.

But we can't leave our happy Babylonians surveying their Hanging Gardens without touching upon that other garden. The Garden. The original one. The Garden of Eden.

If Amytis and Nebuchadnezzar are imagined happy after the construction of the Hanging Gardens, we must know that Eve and Adam's life in the Garden of Eden was beyond happy. It was idyllic. They had all they could ever want. In fact, they didn't even know what want and longing were!

And then. One fine, perfect Edenic day Eve was out walking. The serpent Satan asked her how she was doing.

"Fine," said the first woman. "I'm just perfectly fine."

The crafty one asked her, "But you can't eat of all the trees in the garden, can you? How can you be fine if there is one thing that you'll never know. And, I guarantee, that the fruit on that tree is the best, Eve. That fruit from the Tree of the Knowledge of Good and Evil is like none you've ever tasted. Are you sure God won't allow you to taste it?"

Eve should have fled, but she stayed to chat. "Well, we are allowed to eat from every other tree. So what's the big deal? But, yes, God said that we couldn't eat of that tree." She looked at the silent serpent and lied, "And He said we can't even touch it."

"You can't eat it or touch it even? Don't you think that's silly, Eve. It's only a tree."

The serpent sidled closer. "What harm could come from eating or, as you say, touching a little tree?"

Eve blurted out, "'Cause He said we'd die if we did that!" She was tempted to run to Adam, but she was curious about what the serpent would say about that death threat.

The snake drew himself up as tall as he could. Right into her perfect ear he whispered, "You will not die. That's not true. The reason God doesn't want you and Adam to eat that fruit is because He doesn't want you to become like He is. He knows everything. The fruit of that tree gets into you and then you, too, will know good and evil. You will be like Him. He wants you to stay innocent. Can't you see how He's playing you, Eve?"

"What do you mean 'know everything'?" Eve turned to look at the tree.

"Everything. Just everything." The serpent slithered over to the tree. "Look, Eve, have you ever seen the beauty of this fruit? And I've eaten it. It's the best-tasting fruit of them all. It is. Would I lie to you?"

Eve snapped a perfect piece of the fruit off and held it in her hand. It is exquisite, she thought. Exquisite. And he says it's the best-tasting of all the fruits. She turned it over and over in her perfect hand. Why should we be denied anything, she asked herself. I do want to know everything God knows. I do want to know what that thing called good is. And, also, what is evil? I want to know.

Eve took the pretty fruit and with her perfect hand put it to her perfect mouth.

She gave it to her perfect husband and he ate it.

They looked at each other and fled from their naked shame and their God. Fled down the long, dark corridors of history. Fled. Fled.

They say that if you look real hard into the Iraqi desert on a black and starlit night you can see "a flaming sword flashing back and forth," back and forth across the biting, wind-swept sands.

FOR BEST RESULTS THIS GARDEN SHOULD
BE PLANTED EVERY DAY

Five rows of "P" eas:
Preparedness.
Promptness.
Perseverance.
Politeness.
Prayer.

Three rows of Squash:
Squash gossip.
Squash criticism.
Squash indifference.

Five rows of Lettuce:
Let us love one another.
Let us be faithful.
Let us be truthful.
Let us be unselfish.
Let us be Godly.

Three rows of Turnips:
Turn up for church.
Turn up with a new idea.
Turn up with the determination to do a
Better job tomorrow than you did today.

UBI SUNT AND OTHER CONSIDERATIONS

The twentieth century since the birth of Jesus Christ is over. Most of us were alive to blow a kiss to the last one thousand years and to give a tentative hug to the next.

The last people to enter a new millennium were firmly rooted in the Dark Ages. 1000 A.D. dawned on a Europe where the feudal system pinned everyone in place. You were serf or you were a keeper of serfs. Most of the serfs and the noble class were illiterate, lived lives of quiet desperation and loved and lost amid wars and rumors of wars. But there were flowers and farms and fruits of feudal labor.

The Ages of Renaissance, Exploration, Enlightenment, Science, Industry and Space define the 1,000 years since the Dark Ages. But who standing by the water clock in a cloister in Paris on the eve of 1000 A.D. could have ever envisioned what the second millennium would carry in its time capsule? Who now on the threshold of the third millennium can fathom its depths?

But there are constant things. Love endures. Hope springs. Faith persists. And the flowers bloom like they have since the Beginning. The trees spring forth. The birds sing. The earth endures.

In the 20th century America had a love affair with flowers. And like earliest man we picked them and arranged them and ornamented ourselves and our environments with them.

From 1900 to 1910 we were still firmly rooted here in America in the Victorian Age. Horses and buggies meandered down shady lanes where ladies with big hats and long dresses clung to the arms of men with dirty spats on their shoes. But America was becoming "Amerika" to hundreds of thousands of immigrants who came to our shores seeking El Dorado. We were a rather provincial people perched on the threshold of an urban century.

By the time Queen Victoria ascended the throne of England in 1837, most of the flowers we work with today were in cultivation. The Victorian's love of flowers caused them to group as many as they could into any bouquet. They had clear preferences for containers: "Bronze or black vases, dark green, pure white or silver, always produce a good effect, and so does a straw basket, while clear glass, which shows the graceful clasping of stems, is perhaps prettiest of all." St. Nicholas Magazine

It was during Victorian days that the dahlia, the gladiolus and the pansy took precedence over the tulip and auricula as favorite florist's flowers. From the little Johnny jump-ups, Henry Dreer of Philadelphia produced the varieties of pansy so beloved by Victorians and moderns.

In the second decade of the last century we loved the Romans and Greeks---again. August 24, 79 A.D. the top of Mt. Vesuvius blew apart in a volcanic explosion. Twenty-eight hours later two cities, Pompeii and Herculaneum, had ceased to exist. They were buried in tact under volcanic ash and lava. In the late nineteenth century and in the decade between 1910 and 1920, archaeologists dug sporadically at the two sites. The discoveries of mosaics, homes, everyday objects and lava-preserved people sparked a renewed interest in Rome and Greece.

The neo-Classic flower arrangement favored in the 20's used a profusion of plant materials (often culminating in a steeple effect). The containers were decidedly in the Roman and Greek styles and often looked like urns and had Roman scenes or faces on them. The Classic cultures were back again as they had returned during the Renaissance in Europe.

But our second decade was not to languish in antiquities. In 1914 the West entered the only global war ever fought in man's history. We emerged from World War I and the second decade of the new century forever changed---older but not wiser as the following years would reveal.

The 1920's were several weeks old when the 18th Amendment (Prohibition) outlawed "the manufacturing, selling, bartering, transporting, importing, exporting, delivering, furnishing or possessing of any intoxicating liquors." What President Hoover called "a great social and economic experiment, noble in motive" ended in wholesale breaking of the law by ordinary citizens and the firm establishment of the Mafia in America.

In the suburbs, on stoops and outside fire escapes window boxes and flowers flourished throughout the very wet, roaring twenties. "Hooch" bottles held posies on the sink beside the bathtub gin. This confused and lawless decade ended with the Stock Market Crash on October 29, 1929 when everyone had to take off those rose-colored glasses.

The Great Depression that followed the Crash of '29 dominated the decade of the 1930's. Decent, able-bodied citizens were forced into bread lines and sold apples on street corners to support their families. Broken and broke men rode the rails from town to town and begged at backdoors for a meal. These hoboes were not the only ones in need. "Buddy, can you spare a dime?" echoed down the streets and byways of America.

The five-and-ten cent stores came of age in the 1930's. They sold cheap, useful wares to people with limited income. Depression Glass is the name given the colored glassware made during these lean years. The glass was turned out in great quantity and sold through dime stores or given away as promotions or inducements to buy other products.

Home-grown roses, daisies, rudebeckia and nasturtiums sold by the needy on street corners were brought home and put in a tumbler or vase of this pink, green, blue, red, amber or clear glassware.

America in the thirties, reeling from World War I, the roaring Twenties, the Crash and the Depression was too benumbed to hear the sound of goose steps across the ocean.

The 1940's had barely begun when on December 7, 1941 the Japanese bombed Pearl Harbor. World War II had begun. Rosie the Riveter left her home and manned the factories while our men left for theatres with foreign names: Iwo Jima, Morocco, Anzio, Guadalcanal.

Perhaps the contrast between the destruction and desolation of war and the order and peacefulness of a water garden is what drew us to this unique type of arrangement in the '40's. Pond and lake plants have always fascinated---plants growing and blooming in a water medium. In the water garden two distinct elements meet and meld to create a quiet, disparate beauty. A water garden is best displayed when it is part of another design such as a rose, iris or wild garden. Place the water garden where it will get sun, away from deciduous trees. It should be sheltered from cold winds and in a low part of your garden because water seeks the lowest level. Some flowering plants for a water garden are: floating heart, true forget-me-not, water hyacinth, water-poppy, water-snowflake and, of course, the water lily. The 1940's fell in love with these unusual gardens.

"When The Lights [Went] On Again All Over The World" in 1945, the post WW II generation adopted the slogan of Satchel Paige: "Don't look back. Something might be gaining on you."

In the rock 'n roll, Father Knows Best climate of the 1950's the pacific Oriental style arrangement of flowers became all the rage with garden clubs and flower shows. The Oriental Manner had been practiced in America prior to World War II, but since the '50's the Japanese style has become standard in US flower shows and homes.

The Oriental Manner is a line arrangement. The observer is always considered "the sun" looking down on the triangle lines of heaven, earth and man. Favorite flowers for such an arrangement are the chrysanthemum, orchid, iris, paper-white narcissus and the red and white camellia. Flowering branches are often used as are branches of pine and cypress. Bamboo and grasses stand alone or are combined with other plant material.

The Fabulous Fifties was the decade of television, the jitterbug, the Korean War, suburbia, barbecues and the McCarthy hearings. Fads as divergent as the hula hoop and bomb shelters competed for the public's attention.

In this decade we definitely heard the Red Bear roaring in his distant northern den.

Out of the carefree Fifties, the Sixties roared in like a freight train loaded with sloganeers: "Life is free. Quit now!" "Peace, Love, Nickel Bag." "Make love not war!" "Freedom Now!" We were a nation of rebels with causes: the Black Revolution, the Drug Revolution, the Sex Revolution, the Protest against the war in Vietnam, the Feminist Revolution, the Gay Revolution. We were mixing it up and spitting it out.

The chaos and boldness of the 1960's created stunning, unusual and/or ridiculous art forms. Flower arrangements were influenced by Op Art and Andy Warhol's Pop Art Movement. Kale and broccoli mingled with Bird of Paradise and grapes in arrangements designed to shock and to astonish.

"Do Your Own Thing" reigned in flower shows and on the streets. This turbulent decade ended with an impending impeachment of a President and with a populace wrung out, strung out and confused.

In the 1970's we began to return to the earth for security and because she was showing signs of neglect. What better way to revere her than to have a plot of earth on our coffee tables and beside our hearths?

A London physician, Dr. Nathaniel Ward, planted the egg of a Sphinx moth in garden soil inside a closed glass container. As the egg matured, he noticed that seeds in the soil not only germinated but were thriving in this airless container. The moth matured and died, but the plants lived four years in the Wardian box. Thus in 1829 a revolutionary method of growing and enjoying indoor plants was born. Today we call his "box" a terrarium. We loved terrariums in the '70's.

Small perfume bottles and large water coolers as well as all the pickle jars and snifters and wine bottles in between can and have been used for terrariums in the last 150 years. Ferns, ivies, cactus, succulents and flowering houseplants will thrive in a terrarium. If you missed this indoor gardening fad in the '70's, definitely plant one now.

The Ecology Movement was born in the Seventies. Over the decades we had learned that we cannot trust man. Better take care of faithful Mother Earth.

"Renew and recycle." The 1980's revamped the way we "do" garbage. No matter that the garbage men were dumping offshore and syringes and bloody bandages were pocking our beaches. No matter that business and industry didn't want the plastic or the glass and formidable mountains of the stuff were piling up in obscure places for future archaeologists to find and to ponder. We wanted to recycle and we recycled.

Flower arrangements made of old plastic, "found" materials, Thrift Shop treasures and curbside snatchings got Blue's at the best flower shows.

Paint them, spray them, polish them, fasten them together and you're an artist. We still would put posies in vases, but we loved those "one man's junk is another man's treasure" creations.

The 80's closed with a mini-Crash, a lot of solid, middle-class people chopped from Blue Chip companies and a country decidedly in a no-nonsense mood.

The 1990's logged on with a new elite in charge: Cyberspaceniks.

Who knows? In this new millennium we could be back to where we were in 1000 A.D. That society had nobles and serfs. This new two-tiered society could be made up of Cyberspaceniks and the rest of us. Information rules. There are the Cognescenti and the non-Cognescenti.

Perhaps in this new century we will only cogitate about or contemplate flowers. Perhaps in this brave new world the Cognescenti will find a way to compute flowers or to offer them in bytes rather than in bouquets.

In the decades of the Twentieth Century we have gone from bustles to bikinis, from the buggy to satellite bugging systems, from crystal sets to computers, from a world with many cultures to the great Global Village. We have experienced more and advanced technically more from 1900 to 2000 than in any other one hundred-year period in man's long recorded history.

But I cry, "Ubi sunt?" Where are they?

Where have all the flowers gone?

Where have we gone and where will we go?

So much change, so much uncertainty, so much to fear and to hope for.

Ubi sunt? Where are we going?

Who knows in this millennium what Aquarius will spill from his earthen jug? It's comforting to know that in addition to disposable diapers and styrofoam cups, faith, hope and love will endure.

And, of course, the flowers of the field will endure and re-bloom and re-new the earth and our spirits.

If those things endure, I think that's enough. Don't you?

THE GARDENER'S ALPHABET

A for Achillea yellow, ferny, tall.
B for Bluets dainty, creepy, small.
C for Centaurea and all bachelor's buttons.
D for Day Lily, prize for gluttons.
E for Euphorbia milky, chartreuse green.
F for Filipendula pink against my screen.
G for Gaillardia and all daisies of the world.
H for Hibiscus furled or unfurled.
I for Iris bearded or not.
J for Japanese beetles winged or caught.
K for Kew Brooms, Kalanchoes and Kochias.
L for spiky Liatris and the cardinal Lobelias.
M for Monarda where bees go to die.
N for Nepeta where cats go to sigh.
O for Oenothera invading all my beds.
P for Poppies with their Papaver paper heads.
Q for Queen Anne's Lace crocheted, regal and white.
R for Red Hot Pokers poking through the night.
S for Solomon's Seal wizened in the wood.
T for Trillium and her tri-petaled hood.
U for Uvularia, merry bells tolling Spring.
V for Verbascum and her basal rosette ring.
W for the wild Weeds which we all descry.
X for iXia for my rhyme too much "I."
Y for yearning Yarrow which brings us back to A.
Z for Zantedeschia. Now I'll say, "Good day."

About the Author

Sandra Sweeny Silver is a prolific researcher, writer of fiction and non-fiction and lecturer on a variety of topics from ancient history and religion to gardening and cooking. She has published three other books as well as written numerous articles and reviews. She lives in Connecticut and Naples, Florida with her husband Steve. Her greatest loves are her faith and her family who inspire and infuse all of her work.

Printed in the United States
78453LV00005B/148-153